KT-148-675

RACE RELATIONS IN PRISONS

Race Relations in Prisons

ELAINE GENDERS AND ELAINE PLAYER

With the Assistance of

VALERIE JOHNSTON

Centre for Criminological Research,
University of Oxford

GLASGOW UNIVERSITY
LAW LIBRARY

CLARENDON PRESS · OXFORD
1989

Oxford University Press, Walton Street, Oxford OX2 6DP
Oxford New York Toronto
Delhi Bombay Calcutta Madras Karachi
Petaling Jaya Singapore Hong Kong Tokyo
Nairobi Dar es Salaam Cape Town
Melbourne Auckland
and associated companies in
Berlin Ibadan

Oxford is a trade mark of Oxford University Press

© Crown Copyright 1989

Published by permission of the Controller of Her Majesty's Stationery Office

All rights reserved. No part of this publication may be reproduced,
stored in a retrieval system, or transmitted, in any form or by any means,
electronic, mechanical, photocopying, recording, or otherwise, without
the prior permission of Oxford University Press

British Library Cataloguing in Publication Data
Genders, Elaine
Race relations in prisons.
1. Great Britain. Prisoners. Race relations
I. Title II. Player, Elaine III. Johnston,
Valerie
365'.6
ISBN 0–19–825617–5

Library of Congress Cataloging in Publication Data
Genders, Elaine.
Race relations in prison.
1. Prisons and race relations—England. I. Player,
Elaine. II. Johnston, Valerie J., 1951–
III. Title.
HV9640.E5G46 1988   365.6   88–25344
ISBN 0–19–825617–5

Typeset by Cambrian Typesetters, Frimley, Camberley, Surrey
Printed and bound in Great Britain by Biddles Ltd.
Guildford and King's Lynn

LAW

Acknowledgements

RACE relations in prisons is largely uncharted territory in British criminology. Our research represents a preliminary exploration of the field. In designing the study it became apparent that the scope of the subject was so wide, and the issues so complex, that clearly defined limits would have to be set. We decided to opt for an in-depth study of three institutions, rather than spreading the research more thinly across a greater number, and broader range, of establishments.

The study was commissioned and funded by the Home Office Research and Planning Unit, which in 1984 took up the suggestion of Dr Roger Hood that a study of race relations in prisons should be carried out at the Centre for Criminological Research. A special debt of gratitude is owed to Roger Hood, who from the outset has expressed a keen interest in the project. He has played an important role in helping us to clarify our arguments and present our findings in a straightforward and, we hope, intelligible form. But perhaps his greatest contribution was his persistent encouragement to us to get the manuscript completed. For all this we thank him.

We are especially grateful to Roy Walmsley of the Home Office Research and Planning Unit for easing the passage of this research with tact and good humour, and also to his colleague John Ditchfield. At the outset of our enquiry we were enormously encouraged by the open-mindedness and vision of Philippa Drew, who at that time was the head of P3 Division of the Prison Department. Her successor, Tony Butler, has been approachable and supportive, and has continued to demonstrate his personal interest in, and the department's commitment to, the research and its publication. Others members of the division who have been helpful in ways too numerous to mention are Trish Atkins and Keith Bannister.

The study would not have been possible without the co-operation and tolerance of the staff and inmates at the three main establishments who met our many requests for assistance with good humour and who stoically endured our barrage of questioning. Likewise, we wish to thank inmates and staff at the two other establishments who facilitated our brief visits to them. Pseudonyms have been given to all five institutions in order to ensure the anonymity of those individuals who took part in the research.

We are also grateful to members of the Regional Race Relations Co-ordinators Group for allowing us to attend their meetings; to members of the Boards of Visitors at the five establishments; and to the staff tutors on the generic course at Holly Royde, Manchester.

We are indebted to Peter Laing, Liz Lockey, and Yasmin Khan of the Commission for Racial Equality for their support and encouragement throughout the research and for their valuable comments on our Interim Report. Professor Juliet Cheetham also gave us some valuable advice.

We benefited from a diligent and enthusiastic Steering Committee, who did their best to keep us on the right track. In particular, we thank our academic advisors, Professor John Rex and Dr Mansur Lalljee, from whose knowledge we have gained enormously and from whom we have drawn considerable moral support.

We were fortunate to find someone as resilient as Valerie Johnston, who for three months painstakingly traipsed around eight prisons with a not-so-portable computer, and undertook the statistical study of Standard Classification Forms. Her willingness to go well beyond the call of duty has been exploited on more than one occasion.

We are grateful to colleagues at the Centre for their moral support, and to Georgina Marson, Kaye Bewley, and Vivien Chamberlain for the care and effort they have demonstrated in preparing and proof-reading the manuscript. Last but not least, many thanks to our families and friends, who kept the home fires burning, and to each other for being there.

The views expressed are those of the authors and not necessarily those of the Home Office or any other government body or department.

E. G.
E. P.

Contents

1

Approaching the Study of Race
Relations in Prisons

1. WHY STUDY RACE RELATIONS?

Race relations is a subject which has been notably absent from
research into British prisons. Important empirical studies, such
as *Pentonville* and *Albany*, which were carried out in the 1960s
and 1970s made no reference to the effects of racial differences
upon the social organization of these prisons.[1] One explanation
is that the presence of substantial numbers of different racial
groups in the prison population is a relatively recent phenomenon.[2] It was only in June 1986 that a Home Office Statistical
Bulletin was published which revealed, for the first time, the
ethnic composition of the prison population for England and
Wales.[3] These figures confirmed what had been suspected by
observers inside and outside the prison system, namely that
Black people were substantially over-represented amongst both
the remand and sentenced populations in custody.

The Statistical Bulletin showed that although people of West
Indian or African origin constitute less than 2 per cent of the
general population, they represented, on 30 June 1985, 8 per
cent of the 45,926 men and 12 per cent of the 1,577 women in

---

[1] T. P. Morris, P. Morris, and B. Barer (1963), *Pentonville: A Sociological
Study of an English Prison* (London: Routledge and Kegan Paul), R. D. King
and K. W. Elliott (1977), *Albany: Birth of a Prison—End of an Era* (London:
Routledge and Kegan Paul).

[2] This research has been concerned with prisoners who fall within three
broad racial categories: those of Caucasian descent, those of Afro-Caribbean
descent, and those of Indo-Asian descent. Throughout the text these groups
are referred to as 'Whites', 'Blacks', and Asians', respectively.

[3] Home Office (1986), *The Ethnic Origin of Prisoners: The Prison Population
on 30th June 1985 and Persons Received July 1984–March 1985*, Statistical
Bulletin.

prisons and youth custody centres.[4] Other ethnic groups were less disproportionately represented. Those of Chinese, Arab, or mixed origin comprised between 2 and 3 per cent of the prison population, but only about 1 per cent of the community at large. Persons of Indo-Asian origin were not over-represented at all, but formed about 2 per cent of both those in prison and in the general population. Caution, however, is required when interpreting these data. The prison population is not drawn randomly from a cross-section of the general public but skews towards working-class males in the younger age-groups who live in urban areas. If these criteria were controlled, it is a matter for speculation whether such a disproportionate representation of Black people would continue. But it was also clear that, in comparison with White prisoners, non-White ethnic minorities were particularly over-represented amongst those remanded in custody and those serving longer sentences. Yet they had fewer previous convictions and were less likely to serve their sentences in open training establishments. The data which are available provide no conclusive explanation about the causes of these differences. However, what they have undoubtedly established is the significance of race for the organization and administration of the prison system.

In the USA race relations remained largely invisible in major studies of inmate subcultures until the 1970s, despite the fact that Blacks, Mexicans, and Puerto Ricans had long constituted sizeable proportions of the prison populations. The so-called 'colour-blind' approach to prison research was replaced only after the serious disturbances led by Black Muslim prisoners in the 1960s and their initiation of hundreds of lawsuits, which heralded a new era of Federal Court involvement in prison administration. During this time there was an increasing awareness that prisoner subcultures were not simply functional adaptations to the deprivations associated with imprisonment but reflected behaviour, attitudes, and beliefs which had been imported from the outside world. The impact of the civil rights movement and the growing politicization of Black people in American society spilled over into the prisons. A number of

[4] Ibid. 6–7. The general population figures were taken from estimates in the 1984 *EC Labour Force Survey*.

important studies testified to the racial polarization which existed in certain establishments and to the proliferation of distinct organizations within the inmate culture, built around racial symbolism and ideology.[5] Race relations in American prisons thus became characterized by avoidance, strain, tension, and conflict. And by the mid-1970s the dominance of racial cleavages was described as the most salient aspect of the prisoner subculture.[6]

The adage that what happens in the USA today will happen in Britain tomorrow is a fearful reminder of the importance of race relations for the prison system. This analogy, however, cannot be taken too far. The development of race relations and the patterns of immigration and settlement in Britain differ in vital respects from those found in the USA. Neither do British prisons share the history of racial segregation which has characterized many American institutions.[7] And there are fundamental differences in the administration, organization, and regimes of prisons in the two countries. But the fact that, to date, prisons in this country have not witnessed major disturbances based upon racial divisions provides no grounds for complacency. Prison society inevitably reflects, to some degree, the wider social order of which it is a part. The inner-city disturbances of the 1980s marked growing unrest among Black youth and, in particular, provided evidence of their disaffection towards, and discriminatory treatment by, some of the agencies of criminal justice. This evidence must be taken into account for those who live and work in the multi-racial environment of prisons.

To depict the social world of the prison simply as a microcosm of society, however, is to deny both the special

---

[5] See e.g. T. Davidson (1974), *Chicano Prisoners: The Key to San Quentin* (New York: Holt Rinehart and Winston); J. Irwin (1970), *The Felon* (Englewood Cliffs, NJ: Prentice Hall) 80–2; J. Irwin (1977), 'The Changing Social Structure of the Man's Prison', in D. Greenberg (ed.), *Corrections and Punishment* (Beverley Hills, Calif.: Sage Publications); L. Carroll (1982), 'Race, Ethnicity, and the Social Order of the Prison', in R. Johnson and H. Toch (eds.), *The Pains of Imprisonment* (London: Sage), 181–203.

[6] Irwin, *The Felon*; p. 80.

[7] See e.g. H. E. Barnes and N. K. Teeters (1959), *New Horizons in Criminology* (Englewood Cliffs, NJ: Prentice Hall); New York State Special Commissions on Attica (1972), *Official Report* (New York: Bantam Books).

characteristics of total institutions and the significance which race relations assume in this enclosed environment. As Goffman pointed out, in outside society members tend to sleep, work, and play in different places, with different co-participants and under different authorities.[8] Yet in prison all aspects of life are conducted in the same place and under the same authority. Each phase of an inmate's daily activity is carried on in the immediate company of a large group of others. Routine activities are tightly scheduled and their sequence is regulated by a system of explicit formal rulings and imposed by a body of officials. Most importantly, there is a fundamental social divide between inmates and the supervisory staff. The hegemony of prison staff and the derogated status of prisoners characterize the structural separation of the two groups, which in terms of its absolute quality, is unsurpassed in almost all social settings in the outside community:

It is hard to imagine a setting which would be less conducive to accommodative race relations than the prison. Its inmate population is recruited from the least successful and most unstable elements of both majority and minority racial groups. Prisoners are disproportionately representative of the more violence-prone members of society. As a result of crowding, idleness, boredom, sexual deprivation, and constant surveillance prisons produce enormous inter-personal tension.[9]

2. RACIAL MINORITIES IN BRITAIN AND THE DEVELOPMENT OF RACE RELATIONS POLICY

Just as race relations in prisons cannot be viewed in isolation from race relations in the wider society, the development of a race relations policy in prisons cannot be understood without recourse to the historical evolution of such measures in the outside world. It is thus imperative briefly to consider the patterns of immigration and settlement of racial minority groups

---

[8] E. Goffman (1961), *Asylums* (Harmondsworth: Penguin).
[9] J. B. Jacons (1979), 'Race Relations and the Prisoner Sub-Culture', in N. Norris and M. Tonry (eds.), *Crime and Justice: An Annual Review of Research* (Chicago: University of Chicago Press), i. 1–28, at p. 23.

in Britain and the consequent development of race relations legislation.

Contrary to popular belief, race relations is not a new phenomenon in Britain. The presence of Black people can be traced back at least 400 years to the sixteenth century, when they were transported from the colonies as valets and servants to the aristocracy. Indeed, by the end of the eighteenth century Black people constituted a sizeable minority of between 14,000 and 15,000 in the British population.[10] Since then, however, there have been other significant waves of immigration.

In the mid-nineteenth century the combination of a rising population and a series of bad harvests led to a major movement of people from Ireland, and around the turn of the century virulent anti-semitism prompted the entry of Jews from Eastern Europe.[11] More recently, in the 1940s and 1950s, rapid economic growth in Britain, together with economic decline in their home countries, led to an enormous surge of immigrants: first from Poland and the Eastern European block, and later from the West Indies and South Asia. According to the latest estimates of the Policy Studies Institute, persons of New Commonwealth origin numbered just over two million in Britain in 1982, and of these about four-fifths were non-White.[12] Furthermore, as many as 40 per cent of this non-White population were British-born and over half of those who were immigrants had lived in this country for more than fifteen years. Britain's racial minorities, however, are not evenly spread across the country but tend to be concentrated in only a few regions. Of particular significance in this respect is the Greater London area. As many as a third of all Britain's Asians and a half of the Afro-Caribbeans live in Greater London, whilst only 11 per cent of the White population live in this area.[13] Indeed, over two-thirds (69 per cent) of the Black and Asian households are to be found in Greater London, the West Midlands Metropolitan County, Leicestershire, Nottinghamshire, Derbyshire, and

[10] E. E. Cashmore and B. Troyna (1983), *Introduction to Race Relations* (London: Routledge and Kegan Paul), 3.

[11] A. Pilkington (1984), *Race Relations in Britain* (Slough: University Tutorial Press), 12.

[12] G. Brown (1984), *Black and White Britain* (The Third PSI Survey; London: Heinemann), p. 2.   [13] Ibid. 32, table 10.

West and South Yorkshire; and even within these regions the Black and Bangladeshi populations, in particular, tend to be concentrated within the inner-urban areas. Yet these areas account for only about a quarter (27 per cent) of all White households.[14] Thus, in most areas of the country there are very few non-White people indeed. It is, however, important to stress that although Black and Asian people tend to be grouped together in certain areas of towns and cities, nearly all of them live in electoral wards where the majority are White, and all live in local authority areas where White people are overwhelmingly in the majority.

Within this context, it comes as no surprise that ethnic minority prisoners are not evenly spread across all penal institutions throughout the country, but tend to be concentrated in prisons situated in particular geographical areas. In keeping with their proportions in the outside community, prisoners from racial minority groups tend to be most numerous in the South-East region, where in some establishments they account for between a quarter and a half of the population.

Although since medieval times measures have existed for British monarchs and, later, Home Secretaries to expel foreigners, it was not until the turn of the twentieth century that the State made any concerted effort to regulate race relations.[15] As the social consequences of immigration began to be recognized, the initial response of government was to devise legislation directed at controlling the number and status of immigrants entering the UK. The 1905 Aliens Act was the result of a long campaign against the immigration of Jews from Eastern Europe and represented an important forerunner of modern immigration control.[16] The powers of the Home Secretary to refuse entry and order deportation were further extended immediately before the First World War by the Aliens Restriction Act 1914, and again in 1919. Ironically, however, as further controls were being introduced in relation to aliens in 1914 the British Nationality and Status of Aliens Act of the same year extended

[14] Ibid. 61, table 22.
[15] P. Gordon and F. Klug (1985), *British Immigration Control: A Brief Guide* (London: Runnymede Trust), 1.
[16] S. d'Orey (1984), *Immigration Prisoners: A Forgotten Minority* (London: Runnymede Trust), 1.

the status of British subject to all inhabitants of the British Empire, which at that time included a quarter of the world.

The period between 1948 and 1957 was an important one in the development of race relations in the UK and was characterized by a *laissez-faire* approach to immigration control. The Labour government in 1948 passed a second British Nationality Act, which conferred the status of British citizen upon everyone born thenceforth within the United Kingdom and Colonies. Importantly, the Act also provided for British citizenship to be passed from one generation to another, albeit only through the male line. The post-war years saw Britain embark upon a programme of rapid economic expansion. In an attempt to alleviate the resulting severe shortage of labour the government began to recruit thousands of foreign workers through the introduction of the Polish Resettlement Programme and the European Volunteer Workers Scheme.[17] But these initiatives did not provide the labour force required. The shortage of labour, however, coincided with developments in certain Commonwealth countries which encouraged their citizens to consider migration to Britain. The poor economic climate at home and the excellent prospect of finding employment in Britain made emigration an attractive option to some who, under the 1948 Act had a right of entry or settlement in the UK. As a result, the 1950s saw an unprecedented annual entry of several thousand immigrants first from the Caribbean and, later, from the Indian subcontinent.[18]

It was not until the beginning of the economic recession in the late 1950s that the social consequences of this mass unregulated immigration began to make any real impact upon British politicians. By this time the number of people from the Caribbean and South Asia in Britain was estimated to be somewhere in the region of 200,000, or 0.5 per cent of the total population.[19] Most were to be found in cities such as London, Birmingham, Manchester, and Leeds, where unskilled labour was in greatest demand. A fast-growing anti-immigration lobby

[17] Cashmore and Troyna, *Introduction to Race Relations*, pp. 45–8.
[18] For a full discussion of this migration see N. Deakin (1970), *Colour, Citizenship and British Society* (London: Panther Books); C. Peach (1968), *West Indian Migration in Britain* (London: Oxford University Press).
[19] Cashmore and Troyna, *Introduction in Race Relations*, p. 48.

gained an increasingly responsive audience and, whilst immigration continued to rise, the Conservative government faced mounting demands for immigration control.

At the same time, however, the increasing racial tensions exemplified in the so-called Nottingham and Nottinghill riots of 1958 prompted the emergence of a completely new, and infinitely more liberal, perspective on race relations. In the view of some politicians the solution to bad race relations was not to be found in immigration control but in devising measures designed to combat racism and eradicate the disadvantages faced by both Whites and Blacks. Such measures, however, were not to reach fruition until the middle of the following decade. Meanwhile, the government succumbed to the pressure of the anti-immigration lobby and passed the Commonwealth Immigrants Act of 1962.[20].

The 1962 Act introduced the first controls on immigrants from the Commonwealth and, as such, marked the beginning of what has become known as the 'numbers game'.[21] Under the Act, citizens of the British Commonwealth who did not hold passports issued in the UK or through British High Commissions abroad had to acquire an employment voucher before being allowed entry. This represented an important milestone in the history of race relations in Britain in that it marked the start of an immigration policy designed not to control immigration *per se* but to control the immigration of Black people.[22] Indeed, it has been claimed that the 1962 Act represented the official sanctioning of racial discrimination and the beginning of institutionalized racism.[23]

The Act had originally been opposed by the Labour Party, and the hopes of the more liberal anti-discrimination lobby were raised with the election of a Labour government in 1964. But, while calls were increasingly being made for the introduction of measures to deal with racial disadvantage in the major cities, the pressure from the anti-immigration lobby continued unabated. The response of the government was to appease the two lobbies,

[20] Pilkington, *Race Relations in Britain*, p. 146.
[21] M. D. A. Freeman, and S. Spencer (1979), 'The State, the Law and Race Relations in Britain Today', *Current Legal Problems*, 32: 123–4.
[22] P. Gordon (1984), *Departations and Removals* (London: Runnymede Trust), 58.   [23] Gordon and Klug, *British Immigration Control*, pp. 5–6.

both, ironically, in the same year. The 1965 White Paper *Immigration from the Commonwealth* (Cmnd. 2739) tightened up the 1962 Commonwealth Immigrants Act by reducing the number of work vouchers available for Commonwealth immigrants. At the same time the Race Relations Act 1965 marked the first official recognition of the need for protective laws to combat racial discrimination and promote racial integration. Although an important step forward, this first Race Relations Act was somewhat limited in scope. It outlawed racial discrimination in 'places of public resort', such as places of entertainment, restaurants, hotels, and on public transport; and it set up a Race Relations Board to receive complaints of discrimination and, if necessary, act as a conciliator.

The two contradictory elements of immigration control on the one hand and anti-discrimination regulation on the other were now firmly established within race relations policy. This dual approach was again apparent in 1968, when yet another Commonwealth Immigrants Act and a second Race Relations Act were introduced. The 1968 Race Relations Act extended the prohibition of racial discrimination to the fields of employment, housing, and commercial services; empowered the Race Relations Board to take cases of racial discrimination to court; and set up a new body, the Community Relations Commission.

The Commonwealth Immigrants Act was passed in the face of a new major surge of immigration. The policy of Africanization pursued by some of the East African governments after independence led to many East African Asians opting to take up their right to migrate to the UK rather than lose their British citizenship. As a result panic set in. As one government minister of the time, Richard Crossman, later commented in *The Times*, 'It was widely felt that our improved majority in 1966 was due to our new tough line on immigration control. That is why as a government we were panicked in the autumn of 1967 by top secret reports predicting a mass expulsion of Asians from East Africa'.[24] The Commonwealth Immigrants Act was rushed through Parliament and became law within a week. Under the Act, people who held British passports did not have the right to enter and settle in Britain unless they had a parent or

---

[24] *The Times*, 6 Sept. 1972.

grandparent who either had been born or adopted in the UK or had obtained citizenship in the UK itself. This Act was later held by the European Commission on Human Rights to be racially discriminatory, since its obvious effect was to allow East African Whites to enter Britain but to restrict the opportunities for East African Asians to do so.[25]

In spite of the new Commonwealth Immigrants Act, 1968 witnessed an increasing enthusiasm for even stricter immigration control. Enoch Powell, in his famous 'Rivers of Blood' speech, graphically advocated halting Black immigration and encouraging Black repatriation. Although following this speech Powell was sacked from the Shadow Cabinet, he received phenomenal public support. A Conservative government was elected in 1970 and a new Immigration Act was passed the following year. The 1971 Act codified the previous legislation and placed further restrictions upon Black immigration.[26] It replaced all existing immigration law and remains the basis of immigration control to this day. Unlike earlier legislation, which divided the world into 'British subjects' and 'aliens', the new Act divided the world into 'patrials' and 'non-patrials'. Patrials were defined as those who had a 'close connection' with Britain, such as having been born, adopted, registered, or naturalized in the UK, or having a parent or grandparent who had obtained British citizenship by these means. Patrials were likely to be of British descent and therefore White. Non-patrials, on the other hand, tended to be Black. Under the 1971 Act patrials were free from immigration control, but non-patrials could enter the UK to settle only if they were considered to be dependants of people already settled here, or if they held a work permit to do a specific job for a limited period. In essence, the Act reinforced the racially discriminatory nature of the previous immigration legislation. It also greatly increased the Home Secretary's power of deportation and made provision for the 'voluntary repatriation' of immigrants.[27]

Throughout the following decade race relations continued to

---

[25] I. A. Macdonald (1983), *Immigration Law and Practice* (London: Butterworths), 10–11.

[26] For a full account of the provisions of the 1971 Immigration Act see L. Grant and I. Martin (1982), *Immigration Law and Practice* (London: Cobden Trust).

[27] Macdonald, *Immigration Law and Practice*, pp. 5–6 and 331–65.

receive considerable public attention. The 1970s witnessed a growth in support for the National Front, which had been formed in 1967 from an amalgam of extreme right-wing movements and founded upon a racist ideology. It adopted as a corner-stone of its policies in the 1970s the repatriation of Black and Asian immigrants. In the 1973 local elections the National Front gained as much as 10 per cent of the vote in a number of inner-city wards, and similar levels were achieved again in 1976–7. During this period the party continued to receive high-profile publicity through its demonstrations and election campaigns.

Under the guise of British nationalism the movement sought to legitimize and lend new respectability to overtly racist behaviour and the public voicing of racist attitudes. An attempt at rational argument focused the debate upon the threat which Black and Asian 'immigrants' posed to the British nation by, for example, taking jobs away from Whites at a time of increasing unemployment. Similarly, the anti-discrimination laws were held up as a threat to the individual liberty of White people by restricting their right to choose whom to employ or what colour of person to sell their home to. At the same time, however, counter-demonstrations were held against this racist fervour, and the numerous violent clashes which ensued were widely reported in the media.

All of this was clearly instrumental in sustaining pressure on successive governments to take action. Two further pieces of legislation were introduced: a third Race Relations Act in 1976 and, later, the 1981 British Nationality Act. The 1976 Race Relations Act was passed in the face of evidence of continuing racial discrimination, and represents an important development in anti-discrimination law. Since it remains in force today the provisions of this Act will be discussed in some detail in the next section. The effect of the British Nationality Act was to redefine the categories of British citizenship. The Act abolished the category of 'citizens of the United Kingdom and the Colonies', created under the 1948 British Nationality Act, and replaced it with three new ones: British citizenship, British Dependent citizenship, and British Overseas citizenship. Although it was not an Immigration Act, the effects of this legislation upon the right of abode of people in each of these categories have been defined by some commentators as protecting the interests of White 'patrials' and reinforcing Black and Asian disadvantage.[28] 'The fact that most of those excluded are of Asian origin and most of those included are of European origin, suggests that new law merely enshrines the existing racially discriminatory provisions of immigration law under the new clothing of British citizenship and the right of abode.'[29]

Throughout its development race relations legislation in Britain appears to have represented piecemeal responses to immediate problems. This is particularly so in the case of immigration control, which dominated the trend of early government policy. In an attempt to promote racial harmony in Britain successive governments have continued to maintain strict immigration control while introducing measures aimed at alleviating racial disadvantage. The net result is a race relations policy which lacks internal coherence by its incorporation of two seemingly contradictory elements. On the one hand, there is immigration control, which is concerned to restrict the status and limit the numbers of immigrants entering the UK and is essentially discriminatory in nature. On the other, there are measures designed to alleviate racial disadvantage and eradicate racial discrimination amongst the population settled here.[30]

The evolution of race relations legislation is to some extent mirrored in the development of race relations policy in prisons. The Prison Department has introduced its own measures to ensure racial equality within prisons. But since it is the courts which sentence people to imprisonment the Prison Department has no control over the numbers of ethnic minority inmates assigned to its custody. This is not to say, however, that the 'numbers game' is irrelevant in respect of the prison system. As will become apparent in the following chapters, although there is no analogy to immigration control within the Prison Depart-

---

[28] Macdonald, *Immigration Law and Practice*, pp. 56–70; Pilkington, *Race Relations in Britain*, p. 149; Gordon and Klug, *British Immigration Control*, pp. 8–9.   [29] Macdonald, *Immigration Law and Practice*, p. 69.

[30] These have included the enactment and enforcement of anti-discrimination legislation; the provision of financial aid to local government areas in which significant numbers of immigrants have settled; and the setting up of Community Relations Councils designed to promote harmonious race relations.

ment's race relations policy, the restriction of numbers and the dispersal of ethnic minority inmates constitute a central feature in the management of race relations within individual establishments.

3. THE RACE RELATIONS ACT 1976 AND ITS APPLICATION TO THE PRISON SYSTEM

The Race Relations Act 1976 makes racial discrimination unlawful in the fields of employment, training, and related matters; in education; in the provision of goods, facilities, and services; and in the disposal and management of premises. The main way in which it diverges from previous legislation, however, is in its definition of what constitutes unlawful discrimination. The 1976 Act defines for the first time two types of racial discrimination which, for the sake of convenience, it calls 'direct' and 'indirect' discrimination. *Direct racial discrimination* is defined under section 1 (1) (*a*) of the Act as arising 'where a person treats another person less favourably on racial grounds than he treats, or would treat, someone else'.[31] The Home Office guide to the 1976 Act states that 'in considering whether a particular kind of treatment of a person constitutes direct racial discrimination it is necessary to enquire: (*a*) whether it was less favourable than the treatment which was (or would have been) accorded to another person and, if so, (*b*) whether the less favourable treatment was on racial grounds'. Under the Act it is not necessary to show that a person openly expressed an intention to treat someone less favourably on racial grounds; it will be possible in many instances to infer a discriminatory motive from all the circumstances in which the treatment was given. Goulbourne further demonstrates through legal case history that it is not necessary to show that race is the sole reason for direct racial discrimination but that it is sufficient if race is a substantial reason.[32] Thus, direct discrimination

[31] Home Office (1977), *A Guide to the Race Relations Act 1976* (London: HMSO), 4, para. 2.3.
[32] S. Goulbourne (1985), *Minority Entry to the Legal Profession: A Discussion Paper* (Policy Papers in Ethnic Relations. 2. Centre for Research in Ethnic Relations, University of Warwick), 3.

need not involve the expression of racialist intent, nor do racial grounds have to be proven as the only motivation.

Indirect discrimination is defined under section 1 (1) (*b*) of the Race Relations Act 1976 as consisting of treatment which may be described as equal in a formal sense between different racial groups but discriminatory in its effect on one particular racial group:

Indirect discrimination arises where a person (the discriminator) applies to another (the victim) who is seeking some benefit from him (e.g. a job) a condition or requirement with which he must comply in order to qualify for, or obtain, the benefit, and where the condition or requirement satisfies all of the following criteria: (*a*) it is applied, or would be applied, by the discriminator equally to persons of any racial group; (*b*) it is such that the proportion of persons of the victim's racial group who can comply with it is considerably smaller than the proportion of persons not of that group who can comply with it; (*c*) it is to the detriment of the victim because he cannot comply with it; and (*d*) it cannot be shown by the discriminator to be justifiable irrespective of the colour, race, nationality or ethnic or national origins of the person to whom it is applied.[33]

The 1976 Act also introduced two new mechanisms for combating racial discrimination. First, it established the Commission for Racial Equality, which replaced the functions of both the Race Relations Board of the 1965 Act and the Community Relations Commission of the 1968 Act. Under the Act, the Commission for Racial Equality is empowered to carry out its own investigations of organizations suspected of discrimination and to require any organization found to be discriminating to change its practices. Second, the Act endows individuals with a right of direct access to the designated county or sheriff courts and industrial tribunals for legal remedies for unlawful discrimination.

Three specific disposals are available to a tribunal or court. Both may issue an order declaring the rights of the parties in relation to the Act to which the complaint relates. In addition, a court may issue an injunction or order to a particular person or organization 'to perform or not to commit, or to cease committing specified acts'; and tribunals in employment cases

[33] Home Office, *A Guide to the Race Relations Act 1976*, pp. 4–5, para. 2.4.

may make a recommendation—and it is only a recommendation—that the respondent take a particular course of action, such as re-employing or promoting the complainant. Finally, a tribunal or court may require the respondent to pay the complainant compensation or damages, the amount being based upon direct financial loss sustained by the complainant, such as loss of earnings, and upon an estimate of other less precisely calculable damages, such as injured feelings[34].

There is, however, considerable uncertainty regarding the extent to which the provisions of the 1976 Act apply within the prison system. The operation of particular services within prisons has been subject to recent legal judgment in the case of *Alexander* v. *The Home Office*. In November 1983 a prisoner named Alexander wrote to the Commission for Racial Equality, claiming that he had been repeatedly refused a job in the kitchen at Parkhurst prison on the grounds that he was Black. The commissioners duly instructed solicitors on his behalf and proceedings were initiated in December 1984 at Southampton County Court. Before the claim could be heard on its merits, however, it had first to be determined whether such a complaint was permissible under the 1976 Race Relations Act. A complicating factor in this case was that a complaint could not be brought under the employment sections of the statute because the work of prisoners was not regarded as work under contract of employment or a contract of services. In any event, the Home Office sought to have the case struck out on the grounds that the Act simply did not apply to the provision of facilities in prison. Thus, it was argued, prisoners do not possess any right to seek legal redress for unlawful discrimination under the terms of the 1976 Race Relations Act.

At the preliminary hearing, however, His Honour Judge Smithies referred to sections 20 and 21 of the Race Relations Act and made his judgment in favour of Alexander. The judgment has been well documented in the Equal Opportunities Review.[35] Section 20 (1) of the Act provides that 'it is unlawful for any person concerned with the provision . . . of goods,

---

[34] In cases where indirect discrimination is found, compensation cannot be awarded if the respondent proves that the act of racial discrimination did not involve an intention to treat the complainant less favourably on racial grounds.

[35] Equal Opportunities Review (1987), Law Reports 15 (Sept.–Oct.), 36–7.

facilities or services to the public or a section of the public to discriminate against a person who seeks to obtain or use those facilities or services—(*a*) by refusing or deliberately omitting to provide him with any of them'. Section 21 (2) provides: 'it is unlawful for a person in relation to premises managed by him, to discriminate against a person occupying the premises—(*a*) in the way he affords him access to any benefits or facilities, or by refusing or deliberately omitting to afford him access to them'. In his deliberation Judge Smithies held that the opportunity of being considered for a job in prison was a 'facility' within the meaning of section 20 (1) of the Act and a 'benefit' or 'facility' within the meaning of section 21 (2). He went on to hold that prisoners were a 'section of the public' within the meaning of section 20 (1) and that a prisoner is a 'person occupying the premises' for the purposes of section 21 (2). The case was duly heard on its merits and the judgment delivered in May 1987 was that Alexander had been unlawfully discriminated against in respect to his application to work in the kitchen of Parkhurst prison. For this he was awarded financial compensation.

Whilst this case clearly represents an important landmark for prisoners' rights regarding racial discrimination, the effect of the decision is limited. In the first place, since the judgment was made in a county court, it applies only to the individual case concerned and is not binding upon other cases brought before other courts. Thus, the extent to which the 1976 Act applies to all social, political, and economic transactions within the prison system remains to be tested. Even if the decision were to have set a legal precedent, problems remain regarding the appropriateness for prisoners of the available legal remedies. The inadequacy of procedures to enforce the 1976 Act has been well documented by McCrudden, who identifies the practical difficulties experienced by complainants, the ineffectiveness of the tribunal system, and the lack of power afforded the Commission for Racial Equality.[36] The effectiveness of available legal remedies in the context of the prison system, however, is even more problematic and will be described in later chapters.

[36] C. McCrudden (1983), 'Anti-Discrimination Goals and the Legal Process', N. Glazer and K. Young (eds.), *Ethnic Pluralism and Public Policy* (London: Heinemann), 55–74.

4. THE RESEARCH

(i) Some Definitional Issues

This research represents one of the first attempts to study race relations in British prisons. But 'race relations' is not a simple concept. In seeking to examine the nature of race relations within the prison context it is first necessary to define and clarify the use of specific terms. Both sociologically and biologically race remains one of the most equivocal concepts of our time. Early attempts by biologists to classify people according to their race resulted in a basic categorization of Caucasoid, Negroid, and Mongoloid peoples. All human beings were considered to belong to one of these biologically distinguishable races. This simplistic conception, however, has lost credibility since the Moscow Declaration in 1964, where a consensus of world experts under the umbrella of Unesco concluded that human population groups constitute a continuum, and that the genetic diversity within groups is probably as great as that between groups.[37]

But this is not to deny the significance of the concept of race. Race is almost universally used as a label applied to collections of people who are perceived as physiologically and culturally distinct. Thus race exists as a sociological concept based upon a popular assumption that segments of the human population can be distinguished by common genetic, non-transferable, and observable characteristics—one of the most typical of which is skin colour. The concept of race subsumes the concept of ethnic group. Within broad racial categories ethnic groups can form on the basis of a variety of characteristics, the most common being nationality, language, and religion. Thus, an ethnic group is a collection of people who are seen to be culturally distinct, whether or not they also happen to be physiologically different from other peoples in the same category. Indo-Asian peoples, for example, may be seen as constituting a single racial group but also as comprising many ethnic groups. In an attempt to avoid a lot of repetition, however, the terms 'racial group' and 'ethnic group' will be used here interchangeably.

[37] J. Hiernaux (1965), 'Introduction: "The Moscow Expert Meeting" ', *International Social Science Journal*, 17 (1).

The term 'race relations' refers to how members of different racial groups interrelate. As such, race relations is highly context-specific, its precise nature varying geographically, socially, and over time. In Britain today, race relations is typically discussed in the context of inequality of opportunity, public order, and social deprivation in the inner cities, where the distinctions most commonly made are those based on skin colour.

In sociological discourse, the concept of race relations is normally associated with tensions and hostilities between different racial groups generated by social, economic, or political inequality.[38] Under such circumstances a 'race relations situation' or a 'race relations problem' may be said to exist. The distinction must be made, however, between what constitutes a race relations situation and what constitutes a race relations problem.

According to Rex,[39] a race relations situation emerges when three conditions are fulfilled: first, one group of people behaves to another group of people in a way which denies them equal access to social resources; second, the groups of people are regarded as unalterable; and third, the unequal relation between the groups is justified by various deterministic beliefs.

Pilkington briefly sums up what these three conditions involve.[40] The first, he claims, stresses the significance of inequality. Although there may be a tendency for groups with different cultures to stereotype and look unfavourably upon other groups, it is only when one group is in a position to impose its definitions on others that the situation tends to be considered problematic. The second condition emphasizes the importance of physical differences. Pilkington postulates that a race is defined in this instance as a set of people considered to be physically different and that such physical characteristics are seen as socially significant. The third condition, he states, insists that the essence of the ideas which justify racial inequality lies in

[38] See e.g. J. Rex (1983), *Race Relations in Sociological Theory*, 2nd edn. (London: Routledge and Kegan Paul); M. Banton (1977), *The Idea of Race* (London: Tavistock); Cashmore and Troyna, *Introduction to Race Relations*.

[39] J. Rex (1970), 'The Concept of Race in Sociological Theory', in S. Zubaida (ed.), *Race and Racialism* (London: Tavistock).

[40] Pilkington, *Race Relations in Britain*, p. 11.

the claim that the subordinate group necessarily has those negative characteristics attributed to it.

Within this analytic framework the terms 'race relations situation' and 'race relations problem' may, indeed, be synonymous. But they are not necessarily so and to confuse the two masks an important conceptual difference. Whether or not any given situation or event is regarded as a problem is dependent upon both the context within which it is taking place and the experiences, values, and beliefs of the people confronted by it. In short, what may be regarded by one person as a problem may not be so regarded by another. Consequently, the use of the term *race relations problem* is restricted here to those situations in which prison staff and prisoners might reasonably believe that the nature of race relations is such that it constitutes a problem, either for themselves or for the prison system.

Implicit in Rex's definition of the conditions which constitute a race relations situation is the distinction between the attitudes which members of one racial group hold about members of another and their behaviour towards them. The former provide the conditions for *racial prejudice* which throughout the text will be taken to mean 'a deeply ingrained and inflexible attitude towards specific individuals or collectivities of individuals, incorporating pejorative depictions based upon stereotyped images of them as supposed members of a particular racial group'. The concept of *stereotyping* is central to the concept of racial prejudice. A stereotype, as defined by Cashmore and Troyna, is a generalization which involves attributing identical properties to any person in a group regardless of the actual variation among members of that group.[41] It is, they state, 'A mental image held about particular groups of people constructed on the basis of simplified, distorted or incomplete knowledge of them'.[42] *Racial discrimination* denotes the behavioural element of a race relations situation. It has already been discussed in some detail in the previous section and will be taken to refer to 'the act of treating others unequally and unfavourably, either by intent or by effect, on account of their (supposed) membership of a particular racial group'.

There remains one final term which requires clarification,

[41] Cashmore and Troyna, *Introduction to Race Relations*, p. 36.
[42] Ibid. 37.

that is, *racial incident.* It is a term which is commonly used in association with race relations within the prison system, but which has received little attention within the body of academic literature. In the absence of theoretical guidance, a working definition was developed wherein a racial incident will be taken to mean 'a state of conflict between two or more people of different racial origins, which has been either motivated or escalated by words or deeds which express *racial prejudice* or *racial discrimination*, or is believed to have been motivated or escalated in this way'.

(ii) Planning the Research

The study set out with four primary purposes in mind: first, to chart the development, implementation, and reception of the Prison Department's race relations policy; second, to discover the opinions and beliefs held by staff about the state of race relations in prisons, and to examine how they perceive their role and carry out their duties in dealing with a multi-racial inmate population; third, to explore what inmates think about race relations in prisons, how inmates of different racial origins experience imprisonment, and how race affects their adaptations to their sentence; and fourth, to identify those aspects of prison organization and social interaction which inhibit or facilitate the effective implementation of the Prison Department's policy on race relations.

The study was funded to be completed within two years. Given its nature and scope, a considerable investment of time was required to gain the confidence of staff and inmates in order to penetrate the subtleties and complexities of the subject. For this reason it was decided to focus the study on only three establishments. The choice represents an attempt to include a range of different types of prisons, varying in size, function, and the proportion of ethnic minorities in the population.

Littlebourne is part of the dispersal system and is consequently one of the most secure prisons in the country. During the time of the field-work it had a population of about 400, all of whom were serving long sentences of five years or more. Approximately 10 per cent were ethnic minority inmates, spanning a wide range of racial groups, including Afro-Caribbean, Indo-Asian, Arab, and Semitic peoples. Because of the function of the establishment there is a low turnover of prisoners and a recognition by both staff and inmates of the relative permanence and stability of relationships.

At East Bridge, this pattern was completely reversed. The field-work was based in A wing, which acts as the local prison, receiving recently sentenced inmates before their allocation to training prisons. At the time of the research there were over 1,200 inmates held at East Bridge, about 250 of them in A wing. Most of these men were serving relatively short sentences and spent only a few days or, at most, a few weeks at this establishment. The proportion of ethnic minority prisoners was far higher than at Littlebourne, varying during the period of research between 20 and 30 per cent. Relationships at East Bridge were shaped by the transient nature of the population and the limited opportunities for association, both of which meant that staff and inmates had little chance to get to know one another.

Newfield youth custody centre, with a population of around 200, had the highest proportion of ethnic minority inmates of the three establishments. During the periods of field-work between 25 and 35 per cent were non-White, and virtually all of them were born in Britain of West Indian origin. Although many of these young adults were there for relatively short periods of time, the small scale of the establishment, together with its training function, ensured that staff were able to get to know the inmates and adopt a more pastoral role.

In order to broaden the base of the research and to check some of the findings which emerged from the three prisons, short intensive enquiries were made at two other establishments. Duxton, as a long-term youth custody centre, was considered to be an appropriate choice for comparative purposes because it possessed features in common with both Newfield and Littlebourne. At the time of the research, ethnic minorities constituted 37 per cent of the 288 trainees and, as at Newfield, most of these were British-born of West Indian origin. The other establishment at which short intensive enquiries were made was Wilding, which, like A wing at East Bridge, is a local prison. However, its ethnic minority population, which at the time of the research stood at 37 per cent, differed in important respects from other establishments. Within Wilding's catchment area is a major international airport and, in consequence, the prison receives inmates of many racial origins, including a considerable number of foreign nationals.

Conducting empirical research on any subject requires constant vigilance to take account of individual sensitivities, prejudices, and statuses, while at the same time attempting to steer a direct course towards the research objectives. These problems become particularly acute when the subject of the research is as politically charged as race relations. It was discovered that the very mention of the words 'race relations' could evoke intense emotional reactions both inside and outside of prison.

Field-work involving interaction between researchers and research subjects must also take into account the effects such interaction has upon the nature of the data it produces. The fact that the researchers in this study were female and White, and that their respondents were exclusively male and of varying racial origins, must be considered as having important method-ological implications. There will be those who argue that research of this kind is invalid without the input of a Black field-worker. This argument suggests that Black respondents will be more inhibited and less forthcoming in the presence of a White researcher, and that such a researcher will be insensitive to, and therefore incapable of recording, the nuances of the Black experience. At the root of this argument is the assumption that there is a single and identifiable truth that can only be 'known' through a process of shared experience. It is a position which refutes all intuitive knowledge and denies the possibility that what is 'real' may appear in a range of guises, depending upon the angle from which it is viewed. It is not for us to justify or validate our capacity to undertake this research. But it is incumbent upon us to evaluate and reflect upon the impact which our status as White women had upon the process of carrying out the study.

We were aware that our relations with prison officers were significantly affected by our sex and race. The fact that we were of the same race as most of the officers enabled them to talk easily about 'them and us' in such phrases as, 'Well they're not like us, are they . . . ?,' and 'You must see it yourself, our way of doing things isn't theirs.' We were also left in no doubt that officers saw us as middle-class women and therefore, by definition, naïve about the brutal realities of men's prisons. They adopted a didactic approach, which sought to 'put us straight on the ways of the world'. This seemed to lead to a considerable degree of openness on the part of the staff, who saw our presence not as a threat to their opinions but as an opportunity to express them.

It was clear that our presence as outsiders, and as women, represented a welcome change of routine for inmates, and in consequence very few men refused to be interviewed. The extent to which our interaction with ethnic minority prisoners was affected by racial differences is difficult for us to estimate with any degree of accuracy. However, we were not aware of any reluctance amongst Black or Asian prisoners to take part in the research and we were struck by the seriousness and thoughtfulness with which they approached our questions, and by the ways in which they sought to offer a dispassionate view of their experiences. This being said, the fact that 'you never know what you don't know' is as valid for this research as any other.

(iii) The Methods of Research

The field-work was undertaken in two phases. The first, conducted over a six-month period ending in July 1985, concentrated upon interviews with key Prison Department officials at headquarters and regional offices, and with the staff at the three main prisons. An Interim Report was submitted to the Home Office in October 1985. The second phase, from November 1985 to June 1986, focused upon the inmates and administrative procedures. During this period field-work was also undertaken at the two other establishments and a week-long Prison Service training course on race relations was attended. Three distinct but complementary research techniques were employed: interviews, observational methods, and analyses of records.

Semi-structured interviews lasting between one and three hours were conducted with a total of 140 inmates and 83 prison officers at the three main establishments, and with 18 inmates and 18 officers at the two complementary institutions.

Table 1:1. Prison Establishment by Uniformed Officers Interviewed

Littlebourne		East Bridge		Newfield		Total
No.	%	No.	%	No.	%	
30	36.1	23	27.7	30	36.1	83

Table 1:2. Prison Establishment by Race of Inmates Interviewed

	Littlebourne		Eastbridge		Newfield		Total	
	No.	%	No.	%	No.	%	No.	%
White	23	51.1	21	42.0	19	41.3	63	44.7
Black	12	26.7	17	34.0	18	39.2	47	33.3
Asian	3	6.7	10	20.0	4	8.7	17	12.0
Mixed origin or other race	7	15.5	2	4.0	5	10.9	14	9.9
TOTAL	45		50		46		141	

The selection of inmates for interview was based upon a random sample stratified by race, age, and, wherever possible, sentence length. The physical structure of individual establishments inevitably placed additional constraints upon the sampling process. The size and complexity of East Bridge and Littlebourne precluded random selection from their total populations, and samples were therefore drawn from individual wings. At East Bridge inmates were selected from A Wing, which receives recently sentenced men before their allocation to training prisons; and at Littlebourne the sample was drawn from two of the five wings. At Newfield no such restrictions pertained and a standard random procedure was adopted.[43] Table 1:2 shows the distribution of inmates interviewed at the three main establish-

[43] An attempt was made to obtain a cross-section of inmates and staff for interview at Wilding and Duxton.

ments according to their racial origin. Creating racial categories is a methodological headache. The criticism could quite properly be made that in focusing upon the broad categories of Whites, Blacks, and Asians important cultural differences within racial groups were neglected. In response to this, three points should be made. First, although the categories are based upon a mixed definition of skin colour and geographical origin, they have the advantage of being those which the inmates used when describing themselves. Second, the relatively small numbers of ethnic minority prisoners and, in particular, Asian inmates precluded any comparative analysis of individual ethnic groups and necessitated the employment of broad categories. And third, it emerged from the research that cultural differences between the designated groups appeared to be far more significant in shaping respondents' perceptions of the social interactions of ethnic minority inmates than cultural differences within racial groups.

Prison officers were selected to include a reasonably representative cross-section of those who worked closely with prisoners. The staff interviewed were of varying ages, ranks, and lengths of service and they were either currently, or had been recently, working in direct contact with inmates as wing officers. In addition, interviews of varying lengths were conducted at all five establishments with a total of 51 work supervisors, 12 governors, 5 probation officers, 4 education officers, 7 race relations liaison officers, 5 receptions officers, and 9 officers responsible for cell allocation. A group discussion was also held with the Board of Visitors at East Bridge, and interviews were conducted with at least two members of the Boards at Littlebourne, Newfield, Wilding, and Duxton.

At headquarters and at regional offices administrators who had specific responsibilities for race relations matters also became the targets for research interviews. They included representatives of P3, which has overall responsibility for race relations in the prison service; P4, which deals with young offender establishments and women's prisons; and P6, which is concerned with Prison Service training. Regional race relations co-ordinators, members of the Prison Inspectorate, a representative of the Prison Chaplaincy, and the Home Office Race Relations Consultant were also interviewed.

Observational methods constituted the second major approach to field-work and were employed to provide some insight into the daily routines of prison life. Research which seeks to understand practices which are unquestioningly engaged in day after day must be sensitive to the possibility that people do not always say what they do or, indeed, do what they say. Observational techniques which involve a degree of participation in the daily routines provide some protection against this type of inaccuracy. In each establishment, considerable time was spent during the day and early evening in observing and participating in the routine activities of staff and inmates—from lunch-breaks and dart-playing to adjudications and industrial work. The more relaxed surroundings of the staff canteen and the wing office during coffee-breaks provided useful opportunities to develop informal discussions on issues pertaining to race relations. The continuity and informality of these sorts of contact reduced the social distance between researchers and subjects. Although one criticism of direct observation is that the presence of the researcher inevitably inhibits certain forms of behaviour, it nevertheless provides the only way of monitoring processes of social interaction as they naturally occur. Through these means it was possible to gain some understanding of the problems routinely faced by staff in the management of a multi-racial population, and to gather some knowledge of the ways in which they responded to these problems both formally and informally.

Observational methods were also used to explore the practices and functions of a number of institutional boards, including those responsible for the allocation of labour and the induction and transfer of prisoners. The race relations co-ordinator's meetings held at head office were regularly attended, and these provided a valuable insight into the formal and informal processes of decision-making and policy development.

Prison records were used for a variety of purposes. Index cards were consulted to provide information on the ethnic composition of the inmate populations of the individual establishments. Prisoners' records (F1150 files) were used primarily to collect information about the criminal and social backgrounds of the inmates selected for interview, but they also provided a useful means for cross-checking information gained from other sources. Labour allocation back-records were also analysed for all men who were in Littlebourne on 10 April 1986. This made it possible to compare the prison employment histories of inmates of different racial origins for the whole of their period spent in this establishment.

Finally, in order to broaden the base of the research and to provide quantitative data to complement and verify the information gained through qualitative methods, a survey of Standard Classification Forms was conducted. These are documents which officers are required to complete for each inmate sentenced to over eighteen months' imprisonment and are included in the prisoner's parole dossier. The forms fall into three sections and are filled in on the basis of an interview conducted shortly after an inmate's committal to prison, supplemented by information in prison records. The first section is used to gather factual information about the prisoner's criminal, educational, work, and social background. The second incorporates the interviewing officer's assessment, on a pre-coded scale, of the prisoner's likely behaviour in prison and of his training needs. And in the final part, the assessing officer is required to make recommendations about the inmate's security classification and future allocation, along with any other comment he may wish to make. Altogether a total of 1,255 Standard Classification Forms were consulted for 899 White inmates, 233 Black inmates, and 123 Asians who were held in eight prisons in the South-East and Midland regions. This exercise had two purposes: first, to examine the frequency and nature of disparaging or patronizing language employed by prison officers in these records; and second, to explore the operation of racial stereotyping in formal assessments.

2

The Development, Implementation, and Reception of a Race Relations Policy in Prisons

The Home Office, as the department responsible for race relations and immigration matters, has acknowledged a particular responsibility to ensure that all its constituent parts are above reproach in their adherence to the principle of equality of opportunity enshrined in the 1976 Race Relations Act. Since 1981 the Prison Department has issued specific instructions to prison staff emphasizing the importance of race relations for the professionalism of the service. This chapter will explore the development of the Prison Department's race relations policy and the mechanisms available for its communication and enforcement, the ways in which it has been interpreted and implemented in different establishments, and its reception by prison staff.

1. THE EVOLUTION OF A RACE RELATIONS POLICY

One of the principal methods used by the Prison Department to disseminate information from headquarters to individual establishments is the distribution of Circular Instructions. Over the last five years there have been four on the subject of race relations. These mark significant stages in the development of the content and emphasis of the department's policy.

The first Circular Instruction on race relations, which was issued in July 1981, 'passes on some views and suggestions put forward at seminars on race relations for governors and training staff held at the end of 1978'.[1] At this time the subject of race

[1] Home Office (1981), Prison Department Circular Instruction 28/1981, para. 2.

relations was portrayed as a latent or potential issue for the service rather than one of immediate relevance: the Circular was 'to help staff to meet this challenge if and when it arises'.[2] The Circular laid down a number of principles and practices. First, that good community relations must be based upon 'knowledge and understanding of ethnic minorities'. Second, that ethnic minorities must believe that they will be treated equally regardless of 'differences in race, colour or creed'. Third, that minorities 'will not be allowed to exploit such differences to their own advantage'. On the practical side it was suggested that establishments might find it useful to appoint a member of staff as a 'focal point' on race relations matters, to be called the race relations liaison officer. It was made clear that all establishments would be expected to make this appointment unless 'the ethnic minority inmate population was so insignificant as not to require one'. This implied that below a certain threshold of numbers race relations was not likely to be an issue.

The precise role of the race relations liaison officer was not, however, spelt out in any detail until an addendum to the Circular was published in March 1982. This specified five main duties of the officer: to keep as fully informed as possible about ethnic minority groups represented in the prison and about all relevant legislation and instructions; to be available to staff as a source of information; to assist the officer responsible for training on matters related to ethnic minorities and race relations; to bring to the attention of the governor any actual or potential problems and to suggest ways of dealing with them; and to develop contact with outside ethnic minority communities and Community Relations Councils. Despite the scope and demands of these new duties, the Circular nevertheless explicitly stated that they would 'not require any addition to the task list'. Furthermore, the level at which such an appointment was to be made was not explicitly indicated, beyond the 'hope' that the choice 'fully reflects the importance of his role and responsibility'.[3] The Circular Instruction was, however, at pains to point out that race relations should not become a specialist field, of concern only to race relations liaison officers. The

[2] Ibid., para. 1.
[3] Home Office (1981), Prison Department Circular Instruction 28/1981, addendum 1, para. 4.

appointment should in no way 'diminish the responsibility of individual prison officers for good race relations with prisoners in their care'.[4] Indeed, it added a new dimension to the professionalism required of all prison staff. In conjunction with the development of the policy, a range of training courses were set up, the broad aim of which was

to seek to equip staff with the awareness to recognise attitudes or behaviour reflective of, or impinging on, ethnic sensitivity which is inimical to the maintenance of good order or the development of a positive regime and with the professionalism to exert an appropriate influence.[5]

Two years later, in July 1983, a second Circular on race relations was issued, which constitutes the official statement of the department's race relations policy.[6] It embodies a commitment to the principles outlined in the Circular of 1981, but in important respects it marked a significant shift of emphasis and introduced further practical guidance on how racial equality might be achieved.

Race relations was now acknowledged to be of immediate relevance to the Prison Service. No longer was it depicted as a potential issue, or one of peripheral concern to those establishments holding small numbers of ethnic minority prisoners:

Race relations is an issue which concerns us all . . . All establishments are part of the same system, and all—even those which exceptionally may at present have no Black inmates at all—share (currently or potentially) the same problems and challenges.[7]

The new policy statement clarified the concept of fair and equal treatment. In 1981 reference had been made to treating inmates 'on the same basis' regardless of racial or ethnic differences. It was now emphasized that the realization of fairness and equality did not necessarily imply that everyone should be treated in exactly the same way in all circumstances:

It is important at all times to keep in view the basic fact that our prison regime is inevitably designed with the majority principally in mind. A concession, therefore, to the minority will not represent discriminatory

---

    [4] Ibid., para. 6.   [5] Ibid., para. 7.
    [6] Home Office (1983), Prison Department Circular Instruction 56/1983.
                          [7] Ibid., para. 10.

or preferential practice so long as its effect is to bring their experience into line with that of the majority.[8]

The document went beyond encouraging officers 'to ensure all prisoners understand that they will be treated on the same basis', and specifically instructed them about the professional demands which were now placed upon their behaviour. The opening paragraph of the policy statement unambiguously declared that the department was

committed absolutely to a policy of racial equality and to the elimination of discrimination in all aspects of the work of the Prison Service. It is opposed also to any display of racial prejudice, either by word or conduct, by any member of the service in his dealings with any other person.[9]

Derogatory language and allocation to work and training schemes were targeted for special attention. The policy emphasized that certain grossly offensive words such as 'nigger', 'wog', or 'coon' were 'not allowed' to be used by staff towards prisoners. It was also made clear that condescending or patronizing language which differentiates racial minorities from the majority or treats all Blacks as immigrants should be avoided, as well as language which encourages inmates to disparage racial minorities. Governors were urged to ensure that 'as far as is practicable and sensible' all work, training courses, and activities in general were 'distributed broadly in proportion to the ethnic mix of the inmate population'. The policy statement recognized, however, that certain forms of racial discrimination could be perpetuated by inmates of different races opting for different jobs and training courses. It explicitly stated that self-segregation should be prevented where it leads to certain activities becoming regarded as the province of either Black or White inmates. This was regarded as 'fundamentally wrong because it places a racial constraint upon the availability of work . . . leisure, recreation or eating areas.'[10] Notably, there was no mention in this document of the previously expressed concern that ethnic minorities might exploit differences to their own advantage.

The policy statement also emphasised the need to attract more ethnic minority staff to the service and noted that

[8] Ibid., para. 9.   [9] Ibid., para. 1.   [10] Ibid., paras. 15 and 16.

an experimental campaign had been embarked upon. It praised the development of training arrangements as a considerable achievement, and recognized the central role that a continuous programme of education would have to play if the goals of the policy were to be successfully achieved and maintained.

It was clear that the department had taken serious note of the criticism made in the report of Her Majesty's Chief Inspector of Prisons for 1983 that many of the staff appointed to the post of race relations liaison officer had not been of senior rank.[11] The policy statement did not, however, specify a particular grade of staff or a minimum level of seniority, but advised the governor to ensure that the post would be filled by someone 'sufficiently senior' to carry the responsibility. For the first time an attempt was made to identify the wider responsibilities of governors with regard to race relations. They were given the authority to decide precisely what facilities should be made available to ethnic minorities in the context of their particular establishment and its regime, and were charged with 'a particular duty to establish the right tone and atmosphere by personal example.'[12]

The most recent Circular Instruction on race relations was issued in November 1986 after the field-work for this research had been completed. It reaffirms the principles and practices set out in the policy statement of 1983, but recognizes that there is scope for building on this work.[13] An important development is the promulgation of a succint race relations policy statement and a commitment to make it as widely known as possible, not only to staff but also to inmates, Boards of Visitors, and local ethnic minority groups in the community. Indeed, governors and staff are encouraged to 'feel free to make use of the policy statement and hand out copies wherever and whenever it seems appropriate to do so'.[14]

Once again importance is attached to choosing the right person for the job of race relations liaison officer. But the emphasis is now placed less upon staff seniority and more upon finding someone 'who has the confidence of staff and inmates as well as a fund of energy—and the ability to withstand criticism'.[15]

[11] Home Office (1983), *Report of Her Majesty's Chief Inspector of Prisons* (London: HMSO), para. 2.10.   [12] Ibid., para. 12.
[13] Home Office (1986), Prison Department Circular Instruction 32/1986.
[14] Ibid., para. 2.   [15] Ibid., para. 8.

2. MECHANISMS FOR COMMUNICATING AND IMPLEMENTING THE POLICY

The guidance and instructions given to staff on the avoidance of discriminatory treatment have been accompanied by a series of measures designed to promote their achievement. Three broad strategies have been employed: training, monitoring, and management.

The approach to race relations training has shifted over time in line with the evolution and development of the race relations policy. Until 1985 race relations training on a national basis was organized separately for different grades of staff, so that there was one course for governors and another for chief officers, and so on. They were designed primarily to impart cultural and religious information about ethnic minority groups. In 1985 this system began to be replaced by generic courses to which each establishment now sends a multi-disciplinary team. The programme is less concerned with the communication of factual information and more directed towards the active engagement of participants in race awareness training. The curriculum has three main phases. The first is concerned with the legitimation of race relations as a subject for training. Considerable time is devoted to confronting participants' feelings of resentment, antipathy, and indifference to the need for training in this area. Central to this new approach is the recognition that, if training is to produce changes in professional behaviour, prison staff need to be convinced that the Prison Service still has much to learn about managing and caring for a multi-racial population.[16]

The second phase constitutes the information basis of the course. Less emphasis is now placed upon imparting religious and cultural details, and more upon challenging the stereotypic images which participants have about various ethnic minority groups. Formal lectures are accompanied by field-trips to ethnic minority community schemes so that prison staff can gain more knowledge of ethnic minority groups outside the prison context.

The third phase may be described as the action component of

[16] J. Shaw (1985), 'Race Relations Training Seminars', *Prison Service Journal*, July, pp. 8–11.

the course. The team from each establishment is required to develop a plan which it is expected to implement on its return. The plan must deal with specific issues or problems and set out a detailed strategy which places the steps to be taken in order of priority, identifies necessary resources and key personnel, sets a clear timetable, and anticipates alternative tactics in the event of impediment or obstruction. The Prison Service College issues questionnaires to all participating establishments in order to discover how far the plans have been realized and what difficulties, if any, have been encountered.

In addition to the generic courses there is a two-week specialist programme for newly appointed race relations liaison officers. This is intended to provide information about the evolution of a multi-racial society in Britain, the cultural and religious backgrounds of the principal minority groups, the nature of prejudice and institutional racism, and the functions and skills which race relations liaison officers need in order to carry out their task. It has been claimed that this inevitably leads to an examination of personal attitudes and prejudices.

Race relations has also been included in the initial training programmes for officer recruits and assistant governors, and in the various promotion and development courses for governor grades, chief officers, and principal officers. Concern has, however, been expressed by the Prison Service College about the piecemeal nature of these inputs and the risk of overkill. It is feared that certain governors and officers will suffer from repetitive exposure to the same subject-matter as they gain promotion. Yet it is still possible that there may be some governors, at the most senior level, who have not received any formal race relations training. And it is notable that the subject is not included as a formal element in the senior command courses. In consequence, race relations training is currently under review and suggestions for streamlining courses have been submitted for consideration.

Since 1983 each establishment has been required to monitor the numbers of ethnic minority prisoners in its population. In addition they have been expected to keep a careful check on the proportional representation of ethnic minorities in the various work and training programmes and subject to disciplinary procedures. The Circular Instruction of November 1986 added a number of new areas to be monitored. These included units of accommodation, sporting activities, sick parades, and more details of disciplinary proceedings—minor wing reports, governors' and Boards of Visitors' adjudications, and those placed in segregation on Rule 43 (46) or for punishment. It also drew attention to several other matters which require careful review. These include religious and dietary requirements; ethnic minority literature in the library; racial incidents between inmates; discriminatory behaviour by staff; the proportions of staff who have received race relations training; links with local ethnic minority communities; and the ethnic composition of Boards of Visitors, prison visitors, and the Local Review Committees.

The translation of policy into practice inevitably depends not only upon the nature and details of the strategies employed, but also upon the management structures and administrative processes which organize and implement them. The importance of effective management was clearly recognized in the 1986 Circular, which for the first time set out distinct lines of communication and accountability throughout the service. The organizational structure now involves governors and their race relations liaison officers within individual institutions; the four regional offices, each of which has a race relations co-ordinator; P3 Division, which has central responsibility for race relations; and the Prisons Board. The Regional Race Relations Co-ordinators' Group has been set up to function as the primary channel of communication between establishments and the Prisons Board. Under the chairmanship of P3, its membership now includes all four regional race relations co-ordinators; a representative from the Deputy Director General's Office; the Commandant of the Prison Service College; the Home Office Race Relations Consultant; a member of a Board of Visitors; and staff from the headquarters divisions responsible for young offender establishments and women's prisons (P4), and for Prison Service training (P7).

The terms of reference of the committee are: to provide a forum to discuss issues concerning the development of race relations in prisons, including matters which race relations liaison officers have raised with their regional co-ordinators; to disseminate advice and assistance to establishments; and, to report annually to the Prisons Board on progress in implementing the department's policy.

As far as individual institutions were concerned, the 1986 Circular again advised governors of their responsibility for 'establishing, devising and taking action to improve race relations' and reminded them that they were 'accountable to their Regional Directors' for implementing the policy.[17] Further, it suggested that they would be helped in their task by the creation of a race relations management team.

3. PUTTING THE POLICY INTO PRACTICE

At the time this research was conducted the guidelines set out in the 1983 policy statement afforded considerable discretion to individual establishments in interpreting and implementing the department's race relations policy.[18] This was reflected in the different ways in which the policy was pursued at the five establishments studied. For example, there were considerable variations in the grade of staff chosen to be the race relations liaison officers: there were two assistant governors, one chief officer, one principal officer, and one senior officer. Nevertheless, similar criteria appeared to have been employed in their choice. Structural and organizational considerations were taken into account, as well as personal qualities. At all five establishments the men were chosen because, in the governor's opinion, they had sufficient rank and status to be able to command the respect of their colleagues; they had enough spare capacity within their job description to enable them to devote time to the task; they were receptive to the policies; and they were capable of carrying out their duties. Indeed, the race relations liaison officers interviewed showed a keen interest in, and commitment to, their role.

Nevertheless, notable variations existed both in the systems of management and accountability which had been developed to implement the policy and in what had been achieved—the extent and nature of the liaison which prisons had with ethnic minority organizations in the outside community; the provision

[17] Home Office, Prison Department Circular Instruction 32/1986, para. 7.
[18] It was not possible to evaluate the changes introduced by the 1986 Circular.

of facilities for ethnic minority inmates; the nature and extent of monitoring; the provision of training programmes; the extent of direct action to redress areas of potential discrimination; and the initiatives taken to promote 'good race relations'. At Duxton all matters regarding race relations were delegated to a single member of staff, the principal training officer, who acted as the race relations liaison officer. At Newfield, Littlebourne, and Wilding deputy race relations liaison officers had been appointed to assist in the implementation of the policy. At East Bridge, on the other hand, the race relations liaison officer had set up a race relations committee, which was attended by staff representatives from all wings and by various departments such as education, probation, chaplaincy, and prison industries, as well as members of ethnic minority organizations from the outside community.

The provision of facilities to meet the needs of ethnic minority inmates and the nature and extent of contacts with outside ethnic minority groups were inevitably contingent upon the ethnic composition of the inmate population and the geographical location of the prison. Arrangements had been made at all five establishments for ethnic minorities to be represented on the Boards of Visitors and for religious leaders to visit on a regular basis in order to conduct services. Efforts had also been made to ensure that libraries, kitchens, and canteens catered to some extent for the cultural preferences and religious needs of ethnic minority inmates.

Significantly less success was experienced in establishing and maintaining relationships with ethnic minority groups outside the prison. This was particularly acute where establishments were located at some distance from major urban areas with high ethnic minority populations. Thus, at Newfield, situated in a commuter greenbelt, contacts were restricted to the local Community Relations Council. And Littlebourne, in its rural county setting, was dependent upon ethnic minority contacts in a major urban conurbation some twenty-five miles away. Virtually all contact with groups such as the Sikh Temple and the Indian Community Association involved prison staff arranging meetings outside the prison. East Bridge, in its urban setting, was the only place to receive regular visits from representatives of local ethnic minority groups.

Other variations in the implementation of the policy largely reflected the different ways in which individual race relations liaison officers perceived their roles. At Duxton he had taken a high-profile 'proactive' approach. He regularly monitored the ethnic composition of the inmate population and their representation in different wings, their allocation to different jobs, and the proportion subject to disciplinary proceedings. The race relations 'package' which he had developed for local staff training not only imparted the Prison Department's policy and information about the religious and cultural needs of different ethnic minority groups, but also encouraged participants to question the bases of racial stereotyping and discrimination. He was vigilant in his opposition to the use of racist language and he challenged the under-employment of Black inmates in some work tasks. He had also attempted to promote better race relations amongst inmates by inviting a Black band to give a concert in the prison.

At Newfield the race relations liaison officer took a similar approach. He described his role as providing information on matters of race relations and saw himself as a motivating force in 'promoting awareness and confronting the structural perceptions held by Whites of Blacks'. He placed both practical and symbolic value upon having a reputation for vigilance and upon being seen to take action against racial prejudice and discrimination, whether perpetrated by staff or inmates. A relatively comprehensive monitoring programme had been developed, but race relations was absent from local staff training owing, it was said, to lack of time and resources.

The most important and innovative action taken at Newfield was the circulation to staff and inmates of a local policy statement on race relations, which had been signed by the governor and by the chairman of the local branch of the Prison Officers' Association. This clearly located the responsibility for race relations with both staff and inmates, and trainees were informed of the channels they should take if they wished to make a complaint about race relations.

In contrast, the race relations liaison officer at Littlebourne adopted a low-profile and reactive approach. He had not officially informed staff or inmates about his appointment. He defined his role as the 'eyes and ears of the establishment' and as the 'governor's watchdog on the general climate of social relations'. His major concern was that he should be regarded as neither the 'champion of the Blacks' nor the 'champion of the Whites'. The race relations element in local staff training was restricted to imparting information about the official policy. There was no regular analysis of the representation of inmates of different ethnic origin allocated to different jobs in the prison, and even the ethnic composition of the inmate population was monitored only spasmodically. This officer's efforts were directed towards making himself as fully aware as possible of the religious and cultural needs of the wide range of ethnic minority inmates within his establishment. He made special efforts to attend courses and to maintain close links with Black and Asian community groups outside the prison. Despite this low-profile approach, management at Littlebourne had sought to demonstrate its commitment to good race relations by issuing a local policy statement. But, in contrast to Newfield, this had not been made available to inmates.

The roles of the race relations liaison officers at Wilding and East Bridge were largely determined by the size, composition, and transient nature of their inmate populations. At Wilding, where there were large numbers of foreign nationals amongst the multifarious ethnic minority population, the primary focus was upon the dissemination of information and advice on a wide variety of religious, cultural, and linguistic matters. At East Bridge the difficulties of dealing with a transitory local prison wing were compounded by the fact that the race relations liaison officer was responsible for the whole of this very large and complex prison. Nevertheless, a detailed study of ethnic minorities' representation on various work parties had been completed, and important steps had been taken to develop a race relations training package and to institute regular ethnic monitoring of the inmate population.

4. THE RECEPTION OF THE POLICY

Despite the effort and dedication which had been devoted to the drafting of the policy statement in the Circular Instruction of 1983 and the fact that it was disseminated throughout the Prison

Service, only a third of the officers interviewed in this study said that they had seen a copy of the policy and hardly any of them said that they had actually read it. Virtually all staff, however, were aware that a policy existed and the vast majority of them held firm opinions about it. From the outset of the research it became apparent that the policy statement had stirred considerable controversy amongst prison officers, the majority of whom argued that race relations was not a subject about which a policy should be issued. Comparison was frequently drawn with the 1976 Race Relations Act, which, it was suggested, had created greater racial disharmony by its discrimination against the White indigenous population. The following comments were typical:

They assume that only White people can be prejudiced but I know more Blacks who don't like Whites than the other way around.

The pendulum's swung in the other direction these days, the Blacks have more rights than the Whites . . . A White man can't even sell his house to whoever he wants to these days.

Over half (55 per cent) of the officers had wholly negative views about the policy, believing that the department was simply 'running scared' of the 'Race Relations Board'. Indeed, half of the officers who had actually seen the policy statement argued that the civil servants had gone overboard in pandering to the 'race relations industry'. Only 17 per cent had a positive response to the policy, either believing it to be satisfactory and appropriate or, at the very least, a positive step forward.

Prison officers were, however, far less critical of the ways in which management dealt with race relations within their own establishment. Less than a quarter expressed wholly negative views and over a third held favourable opinions. Yet as many as 40 per cent were unaware that any action had been taken in response to the policy at their prison.

Prison governors and race relations liaison officers generally approved of the policy in principle, believing that some form of guidance on race relations was necessary and that the policy was moving in the right direction. Where there were criticisms they tended to focus upon allegations of lack of leadership from Prison Service headquarters. Cynicism was expressed about the commitment of senior management to its own policy when insufficient facilities were provided to ensure its implementation.

The examples they gave included the absence of time allotted for the work of the race relations liaison officer, and the lack of resources to enable staff to attend local race relations training courses and community-based training programmes. Some governors also expressed frustration about the general tone of the policy document. They felt that a conciliatory and educational approach to race relations was useful and appropriate but half-hearted unless supported by explicit sanctions to combat racist behaviour. Whilst it was agreed that such sanctions would add little to the powers that already existed in the Code of Discipline, it was felt that they would indicate a 'toughness' and 'determination' which the policy currently lacked.

The Prison Department emphasizes the importance of professional behaviour for the promotion of good race relations in prison. Specific guidance has been issued on the use of derogatory language and access to work and training facilities. None the less, there was considerable divergence of opinion about the use of derogatory language. There was a tendency amongst prison officers to argue that language is context-specific and what is 'grossly offensive' in one set of interactions is acceptable in another. How well the individual actors know one another, the nature of the relationship between them, and the accompaniment of other non-verbal gestures all provide a context which, it was suggested, condition the meaning which is given to the words which are spoken:

I call him my little Caribbean Clown and he calls me Snowflake. I don't think it's offensive. I think it's a way of breaking down the barriers. Let's face it, we are different after all.

It was apparent that prison staff held widely differing views about what constituted offensive language and considerable resentment was expressed about the policy guidelines for imposing a particular interpretation of words, such as 'wog' etc. This view was not shared by the administrator at regional offices and headquarters, nor by the governors and race relations liaison officers, who were almost unanimous in opposing the use of racial slang, believing that certain expressions were unacceptable under any circumstances. Only one assistant governor thought that the acceptability of such language was dependent upon the social context.

The attitudes of staff also diverged over the question of whether or not it is appropriate to use language which differentiates racial minorities from the majority. It was asserted that the labelling of racial groups was precisely the same as the identification of any other social group. Hence, to call Black prisoners 'our coloured brethren' is the same as calling Liverpudlians 'Scouses' or drug addicts 'junkies'. Governors, race relations liaison officers, and even administrators were also less condemnatory about this use of language. As one assistant governor said 'I don't know what you can do about this because Londoners are called "Cockneys" and the Welsh "Taffies". Nobody thinks twice about it.' Staff were unsure whether abusive language which had a racial component was worse than abusive language which did not. For example, there were divergent views on whether it is more offensive to call someone a 'Black bastard' as opposed to a 'bastard'.

The policy guidelines on access to work, training, and other activities elicited a mixed response from prison staff. In general, work supervisors and uniformed officers agreed with the principle that all inmates should have an equal opportunity to put in an application and receive fair consideration for a change of work party. Yet considerable controversy was stirred by the directives that 'all jobs, tasks, training courses, and activities generally . . . [should be] distributed broadly in proportion to the ethnic mix of the inmate population', and that 'self-discrimination' should be prevented where it leads to certain activities becoming the province of any single racial group. Almost two-thirds of the work supervisors thought that a policy of proportional distribution was fundamentally wrong. They rejected the constraints which this would place upon their freedom to choose their work-force and argued that what was important was employing 'the right man for the job'. Instructors of training courses expressed anxiety that attempts to ensure an equal representation on vocational programmes would lead to a reduction in standards. They argued that the selection of inmates for training should continue to be based upon enrolling those who were most qualified or able to derive benefit from it. The uniformed staff also feared that a policy of enforcing a proportionate distribution could have undesirable consequences if it denied inmates choice over what they wanted to do and therefore led to resentment and subversive behaviour. Thus, it was suggested that if Black inmates chose to make use of the gym, or if Asian inmates preferred to work in the sewing shop, they should generally be permitted to do so, so long as the resulting build-up of numbers did not threaten the good order of the prison. Indeed, with this caveat in mind, as many as 81 per cent of the uniformed officers thought that staff should not intervene to limit the development of self-segregation.

The dissatisfaction which the uniformed staff expressed, in general, about a race relations policy in prisons, and about the guidance issued on the use of derogatory language and access to work and training facilities, largely dissipated when other specific policy matters were discussed. For example, a majority of staff (71 per cent) were in favour of prison officers receiving some form of training in race relations. Most thought that such training should provide basic information about cultural matters so that staff would be better able to understand the needs of ethnic minority prisoners, as well as becoming more astute in separating the genuine from the deceptive claims of inmates. A significant minority (42 per cent) of officers thought that race awareness training, in which staff would be confronted with their own views, beliefs, and prejudices, would be a useful component in such courses. Although the vast majority of the staff we interviewed said that they had not received any form of race relations training, over half of them said that they would be willing to undertake it and many welcomed the opportunity. This was particularly the case amongst the younger officers and those with less experience in the Prison Service. For example, when officers were asked whether they thought it would be useful for staff to be taught the rudiments of some of the most common ethnic minority languages, only 29 per cent of the over 40 age-group agreed, compared with over 50 per cent of those under 30. Most of those who did not agree based their objections not on grounds of the impracticality of initiating such training, but on the principle that inmates should accommodate to the regime and not the other way around. The majority (68 per cent) of the staff were in favour of recruiting more prison officers from ethnic minority communities. But again the enthusiasm tended to vary according to the length of service of the officer: over 80 per cent of staff with less than three years' service were in favour of this recruitment, compared with 72 per cent of those with medium-length (between three and ten years') service, and 58 per cent of officers with over ten years' experience. In general, the higher the rank of the uniformed officer, the less inclined he was to favour the recruitment of ethnic minority staff. Indeed, three of the four chief officers interviewed felt that there was no need for it.

The case for employing more ethnic minorities was justified by officers largely on three grounds: first, that they would be able to help prisoners of their own racial and cultural background; second, that the control of ethnic minority prisoners would be more easily achieved; and third, that it would illustrate to inmates and staff alike that the Prison Service is not an exclusively White power structure but represents the whole of society. Of those officers who were not in favour of recruiting more ethnic minority staff (32 per cent), about half felt that neither the race of the officer nor the race of the inmate made any difference to the routines of prison life. But just over a third of them felt that the presence of officers from the ethnic minorities would create difficulties since they would not be fully accepted by particular groups of inmates and by certain members of the uniformed staff. This minority view was expressed particularly by officers at Littlebourne, who said that the amount of 'stick' that ethnic minority staff would have to endure from all sides would make their job virtually impossible. It is also worth noting that at East Bridge, where there were both Black and Asian members of staff, White officers commonly expressed the view that the acceptance of ethnic minority staff depended upon their being able to take a joke from their fellow officers about their race and colour.

Most officers were aware that initiatives had been taken by the Prison Department to recruit more ethnic minority staff and knew that these had been largely unsuccessful. They suggested that the reasons for this failure differed for Asians and Blacks. Asian people, they believed, were not applying for this type of employment because they viewed the work as being of low status and outside their traditional aspirations in business and the professions. Black people, on the other hand, were perceived as being ambivalent about, if not hostile to, the work of prison officers and under pressure from their communities to resist becoming a 'flunkey' of the White power structure. But in addition it was apparent that a fundamental presumption existed that people of ethnic minority status were generally less able or qualified, and therefore, if they were to be employed, less rigorous criteria of selection would have to be applied. Hence, despite the general agreement that existed amongst prison staff about the suitability of recruiting more officers from the ethnic minority populations, discussion was almost always preceded by such comments as

I'm in favour so long as they don't drop the standards to let them in.
. . . only if they pass the same tests as everyone else.
There should be no preferential treatment because that's discrimination against White applicants.

The provision of special facilities for ethnic minority prisoners evoked a favourable response from 80 per cent of the officers. Only one in five argued that all inmates should receive exactly the same service. Notwithstanding this overall approval in principle, however, 78 per cent of officers identified certain disadvantages in putting the policy into practice. At the top of their list was the concern that White inmates would define the provisions as special concessions to Black and Asian prisoners and would resent what they considered to be preferential treatment. In addition, staff felt that it was necessary to be ever alert to the possibility of advantage-taking by the ethnic minorities, who would seek to 'manipulate the system for their own benefit'. Finally, dissatisfaction was expressed about the increase in their own workload which the provision of such facilities entailed.

The level of endorsement which the staff gave to special provisions for ethnic minorities varied according to the nature of these facilities and whether or not they were already provided by their own establishment. Facilities which enabled inmates to practise their religion were overwhelmingly supported by the staff, who generally perceived their provision to be a right rather than a privilege. The provision of special facilities, such as ethnic minority newspapers and supplies in the canteen, was also well supported by the staff, but these were generally defined as special allowances to be provided only if they could be procured easily by the establishments. A very different opinion was voiced when officers were asked whether subjects for evening classes should be provided in the most common ethnic minority languages. Over half of the officers were of the opinion that 'when in Rome' ethnic minority prisoners should 'fit in' and participate in the English-speaking classes. In short, staff at all establishments tended to accept the status quo. But they resisted innovations for reasons which could have applied equally well to those existing facilities which they endorsed.

A fundamental issue, which has caused controversy in virtually all race relations debates, concerns the number and distribution of ethnic minorities in the population as a whole. This also raised its head in the prison context. Over 80 per cent of staff believed that the numbers of Asian inmates in the prison population made very little difference to the tenor of race relations. Indeed, only about 20 per cent of staff were in favour of a policy to limit the proportion of Asian prisoners in individual establishments. Interestingly, the majority of these officers were at Littlebourne, where a third of those interviewed thought that a maximum figure should be set. In the case of Black inmates the opposite view was taken. Over 80 per cent of staff felt that the number of Black prisoners in any single establishment fundamentally affected race relations and over half of the officers wanted to see the proportions of Black inmates controlled. These officers argued that where the Black population reached a certain level power struggles inevitably broke out with the White inmates. It was suggested to us that three factors were largely responsible for this type of conflict: first, the tendency amongst Black prisoners to group together; second, the level of noise usually generated by these groups, which makes them highly visible within the prison; and third, the perception of these groups by White inmates as potentially threatening.

Blacks are OK in the singular, but cause problems in groups because they're rebellious and must always have the last word. Whites are not so troublesome.

Blacks group together more than Whites and when they do, they're noisy and intimidatory. And that's what causes the problems because the White lads don't like being put upon by Black groups.

It's only natural that Whites feel threatened when you get a lot of Blacks in who stick together.

However, opinions varied considerably between establishments. Most support for limiting the proportion of Black prisoners was found at Newfield and Littlebourne, where a majority of officers interviewed were in favour of establishing a quota system. However, most of those interviewed at East Bridge were opposed, largely on the grounds that any such system would be unworkable and could result in highly undesirable practices such as 'busing' inmates throughout the system to achieve a notional mix of racial groups. In addition, it is worth noting that older officers with relatively long service tended to be more in favour of restricting the numbers of Black and Asian inmates than the younger, less experienced, staff.

There was, however, no overall agreement upon precisely what constituted the 'ideal proportion' of Black inmates. At Littlebourne, most staff thought that the maximum proportion would be between 10 and 20 per cent, whereas at Newfield the figure was placed at about a third. At East Bridge there was no consensus among the minority who were in favour of any form of quota system. These differences between establishments closely reflected the actual proportions of ethnic minority prisoners which the staff were used to dealing with; and they again signify a general acceptance of what is already familiar. What seems to be indicated, therefore, is that, far from being fixed, prison officers' views and levels of tolerance are flexible. Changes are feared, but opposition is largely dissipated once they have been incorporated into the daily routine of prison life. This must provide at least some modest ground for optimism.

3

Staff Perspectives

The previous chapter presented the views of prison staff about the development and implementation of the Prison Department's race relations policy. The purpose here is to locate these views in the context of the beliefs held by staff about the nature and significance of the racial dimension of prison life. The first part of the chapter explores how far prison staff, and in particular the uniformed officers, considered race to be a significant feature in shaping the nature of social relations in prisons. It illustrates how staff depictions of the different characteristics and behaviour patterns of Black and Asian inmates constitute a system of racial stereotyping, and how this affects their perceptions both of social relations in prisons and the problems of inmates. In the light of these views the latter part of the chapter considers the extent to which prison staff defined race relations as either a problem or, indeed, an issue for the Prison Service. But first, it may be helpful to outline briefly the roles of the various staff groups who work in prisons.

1. THE PRISON OFFICERS

Prisons are complex organizations which are intended to fulfil a number of different purposes and perform a kaleidoscope of functions. A range of staff groups is employed in each establishment to meet the various requirements of the institution and needs of the population. The management structure within individual establishments is headed by the Prison Service governor grades. Civil servants run the administration and civilian instructors are employed in some of the workshops. Probation and education facilities are provided under the auspices of the area Probation Service and the local education authority, and the Prison Medical Service and Prison Psychological Service also provide an input of professional civilian staff. But it is the uniformed officers who constitute the most significant section of a prison's work-force, both numerically and in terms of the centrality of their role. They undertake a multitude of different jobs which vary according to the type and size of establishment. It is possible for uniformed staff to specialize in specific skills such as catering, nursing, physical education, or in building trades within works departments. But by far the majority of officers work as discipline staff charged with the day-to-day care, security, and control of the inmate population. Routinely this entails locking and unlocking prisoners in their cells, ensuring that they are fed, escorting them to and from work, and generally supervising their activities. Most significantly the prison officer is in closer daily contact with inmates than any other member of staff and, in consequence, he provides the main link between the prisoner and the outside world. The officer is typically the inmate's first port of call in gaining access to virtually all facilities. It is through the uniformed staff that inmates book to see a doctor, a probation officer, or make an application to see the prison governor. It is also the prison officer who will give advice on a wide spectrum of issues, from how to get a transistor radio sent in from outside to dealing with a request for a transfer to another prison. But the uniformed staff must also provide the front line of security. They are responsible for the routine searching of a prisoner's cell and his person. They are the men who are charged with enforcing discipline and control, which, in practice, may mean anything from charging a man with a minor disciplinary offence, such as using abusive language, to coping with riots and roof-top protests.

   The officers who were interviewed in this research were representative of all grades and of varying lengths of service and experience. They included young men in their mid-twenties with less than a year in the job, as well as officers approaching retirement with more than thirty years' experience. Perhaps not surprisingly, given the ethnic composition of the Prison Service, all but two of the officers interviewed were White.

2. THE DEVELOPMENT OF RACIAL STEREOTYPES IN PRISONS

Throughout the research it was apparent that prison staff, and in particular the uniformed officers, held in common a number of views about the character and behaviour of ethnic minority inmates and about the ways in which these shaped the development of social relations within establishments. They ascribed to different racial groups distinct patterns of behaviour and different responses to prison regimes and routines; they distinguished the nature of the problems which inmates of different races experienced in prison; and they laid different emphases on the causes of their criminality. What emerged were clearly defined and widely endorsed racial stereotypes which categorized and stigmatized inmates on the basis of the colour of their skin.

The greatest contrast was in their characterization of Black and Asian inmates. Black prisoners were described by all but a handful of officers in at least one of the following negative terms: arrogant, hostile to authority, estranged from the institutions of 'law and order', alienated from the values associated with hard work, and having 'chips on their shoulders'. Precisely what prison officers meant by their assertion that Black inmates had 'chips on their shoulders' was at first unclear and the cliché appeared to encompass a multitude of sins. Nevertheless on closer examination a common underlying theme emerged. In broad terms what they meant was that Black inmates invariably assumed an irrational sense of racial persecution and consequently felt a rancorous antipathy towards White society. More specifically Black inmates were accused of 'seeing racial prejudice around every corner' and 'screaming racial discrimination at every opportunity'. Inside the prison the behaviour of Black inmates was variously depicted as noisy, belligerent, lazy, demanding, and unintelligent.

Only six officers in the entire sample did not refer to Black inmates in one or other of these pejorative ways. As many as 83 per cent of officers at Newfield and East Bridge, and 73 per cent at Littlebourne, specifically said that Black prisoners had a 'chip on their shoulder' and/or that they were anti-authority. Sometimes these characteristics were considered to be innate and occasionally reference was made to the supposed lower position of Blacks on the evolutionary scale:

Let's face it, they're less civilised than us aren't they. (officer)

They remind me of a monkey colony, they keep together in a flock and are always scratching each other's backs and hissing together when they're under any threat. (officer)

I don't like Blacks because they're arrogant and I don't like their body odours. (officer)

Blacks are pig-headed mules—they're the most prejudiced of all—it's their natural way. (officer)

Even the causes of their criminality were thought to differ from those of other racial groups. Although virtually no one attributed White and Asian offending to inherent anti-authority attitudes, a quarter of the officers thought that this was a cause of offending amongst Blacks. Another criticism levelled specifically against Black prisoners was that although they suffered from various social disadvantages in the wider society, in such areas as housing, education, and employment, they nevertheless 'wanted something for nothing' and thought 'the world owed them a living'. Officers argued that although Black inmates aspired to many of the consumerist goals of British society—setting great value, for example, upon money, expensive clothes, and 'flashy cars'—they rejected the conventional means of achieving them, namely hard work and industry:

They've got all the opportunities—what more do they want? We bend over backwards for them in this country. We've been stupid for too long. There's an inbred feeling amongst Blacks that the only way to overcome unemployment and become accepted into society is to commit crime. They purposely set out to commit crime. (officer)

In some instances such views were compounded by references to the 'immigrant status' of Blacks:

They come over here and they think that the world owes them a living. (officer)

Blacks today bear too many grudges—the younger ones don't accept as much as their fathers did when they came over in the 1950s—workwise and housing I mean. (officer)

Black inmates were frequently perceived by prison officers as an invading force, not only in the prison but in the outside community too. It was not unusual for them to believe that Black people constituted as much as a quarter of the British population. As has been mentioned already, over half of the uniformed staff wanted to see a limit set on the proportion of

Black prisoners allocated to any individual establishment and, for a few, this desire was extended to include tougher immigration rules and the enforced repatriation of Black people to the West Indies. In the graphic words of one senior officer, 'Look at us, we fought two World Wars to prevent Britain from becoming a German colony and now we're infested with West Indians.'

In striking contrast, Asian inmates were generally typified by staff as 'model prisoners'. Little concern was expressed about their numbers either in prison or in the outside community:

I wouldn't mind 100 per cent Asians. They're clean, particular and have a great sense of humour. They're fabulous model prisoners. (officer)

If we had a wing full of Asians we wouldn't have any problems. (officer)

Their behaviour in prison was described as unobtrusive, hard working, polite, and mutually supportive. In addition, they were credited with a high degree of intelligence, business acumen, and motivation to improve their lot.

Unlike Black inmates, Asians were not depicted as being estranged from an acceptance of law and order, or from the values of achievement through hard work. Their lives outside prison, within highly supportive communities and closely knit families, were thought to be regulated by a strict moral code which inculcated adherence to law-abiding behaviour. Considerable respect was expressed for their cultures and religions, to such an extent that four out of ten prison officers were mystified as to why 'such strictly controlled' and 'highly religious' men had become involved in crime at all. They tended to see Asian inmates as 'one-off' offenders who were either motivated by a desire to make money in order to set up in legitimate business, or who had committed a violent crime in response to behaviour which offended against the religious and cultural order of their communities. They were not, in other words, 'regular cons'. Thus, although Asian prisoners were described as being culturally distanced from White society because they had retained many of their own customs and traditions, this was not deemed to be incompatible with the social values of British society.

Clearly not all prison officers held these stereotypic images of Black and Asian prisoners. A very small minority ascribed a strikingly different image to Black inmates, characterizing them as attentive to appearance, exuberant, happy-go-lucky, easy-going, and resourceful:

Blacks take a pride in their appearance—they're streetwise and good sportsmen, one thing they can do is their bird. (officer)

They're just naturally effusive, they enjoy life and they don't rush around. They have this easy come easy go attitude and I admire them for it. (officer)

For a very few prison officers Asian inmates represented all that was sly, snivelling, secretive, and manipulative. What is interesting is that, regardless of which stereotypes were applied, staff were clearly focusing upon precisely the same characteristics but interpreting them in different ways. The underlying similarity, for example, between polite and snivelling, insular and secretive, easy come easy go and lazy, and between noisy and exuberant can hardly escape notice. Indeed, this was recognized by a small number of the uniformed and specialist staff:

They're a noisy lot—they dance and giggle and enjoy life——they're born to enjoy it. We sometimes envy their free and easy way of life. If the truth be known, their exuberance interferes with my quiet way of life. That's really what it comes down to. (officer)

We are our own worst enemies. We turn our backs on successful Blacks. A good example is the officers' club. When staff have brought in Black friends in the past the whole place goes quiet. The Black officers we've had here are cracking blokes—nice and intelligent too. We call Blacks arrogant. But we are just as arrogant ourselves. (officer)

Some officers completely misinterpret the behaviour of Black inmates. They prejudge on everything. They think they're loud, mouthy, aggressive and arrogant, when really it's just their cultural exuberance and hot-bloodedness. (officer)

The ways in which prison officers employed racial stereotypes are illustrated in their responses to two particular areas of questioning. The first concerns their descriptions of social relations in prison, and the second centres on their perceptions of the sorts of problems which prisoners experience in prison.

3. RACIAL STEREOTYPES AND SOCIAL RELATIONS

The employment of racial stereotypes by prison officers was most apparent when they discussed the nature of social relations amongst inmates, and between inmates and staff. The important role which race was seen to play in shaping the inmates' social world was first evidenced in the finding that nine out of ten officers noted a definite tendency for inmates of the same race to group together. They did not suggest that such grouping was necessarily founded upon racial hostility, nor did they deny the significance of other factors in group formation, such as age, type of offence, or home area. Rather, they considered that racial identity was a primary factor in shaping patterns of social interaction amongst prisoners, and frequently made reference to the well-worn cliché 'birds of a feather flock together'.

At all three of the main establishments the uniformed staff specified three major advantages which they thought inmates derived from racial grouping. First, they maintained that it could engender a sense of identity, a feeling of belonging, and notions of psychological security. Second, they thought that it enabled members to participate in shared activities and to pool their resources. And third, they believed that it could increase the status, power, and esteem of both the individual a.i.' the group through the provision of 'physical muscle'. However, staff at the three establishments accorded different significance and priority to these functions, and associated different types of benefit with different racial groups. For example, two-thirds of the prison officers at Littlebourne, compared with fewer than one in five at Newfield and East Bridge, focused upon grouping amongst Asian prisoners and identified the benefits accrued to the inmates from this in terms of their opportunities to pool resources and participate in shared activities. At Newfield, on the other hand, where the population consisted almost entirely of White and Black inmates, half of the officers, compared with fewer than a quarter at Littlebourne or East Bridge, associated the advantages of racial grouping with the power, status, and esteem gained by groups of Black prisoners.[1] In contrast, staff at

[1] At Wilding, prison officers' responses were similar to those at Littlebourne—focusing upon Asian grouping and defining the benefits as pooling

all three establishments defined White groups, with the notable exception of the more sophisticated London 'gangsters' and Irish 'terrorist' prisoners at Littlebourne, as relatively un-supportive and disorganized.

But it was in situations of inter-personal conflict that the impact of racial grouping was thought to be most pronounced. Half of the officers felt that when it came to fights and arguments any support offered to a contender invariably came from inmates of his own race. Most importantly, this kind of support was ascribed more often to Blacks than Whites or Asians with comments such as 'You'll never see a Black alone in a fight. If one gets into trouble the whole brotherhood's there.' Other forms of inmate support were thought to be far less dependent upon race. Prison officers who felt that inmates would lend one another tobacco, help write letters, and provide a 'sympathetic ear' to each other were evenly divided as to whether or not this type of assistance crossed racial boundaries.

The significance which officers attributed to race was further reinforced by their assessments of its influence upon staff–inmate relations. Almost two-thirds of the uniformed staff felt that the tendency for inmates to group together on the basis of race directly affected their work as prison officers. The ways in which this was seen to occur, however, varied between establishments. At Newfield and East Bridge prison officers were significantly more likely than those at Littlebourne to state that it made their work more difficult.[2] The explanation for this was that officers at Newfield and East Bridge concentrated upon the grouping of Black prisoners and argued that the support that these groups provided was such that any refusal by staff to meet the demands of an individual inevitably resulted in a confront-ation with the whole 'brotherhood'. At Littlebourne, on the other hand, prison officers focused upon the effects of Asian grouping and identified distinct features of these groups, such as their hierarchical structures and nominal group leaders,

---

resources and participating in shared activities. At Duxton, staff responses again closely mirrored those at Newfield and centred on the benefits for Black trainees who gained power and esteem from grouping.

[2] This view was expressed by 62% of officers at Newfield, by 53% at East Bridge, but by only 24% at Littlebourne.

which were seen to assist staff in their dealings with these inmates.

Apart from the problems associated with racial grouping, almost three-quarters of the uniformed staff in all three establishments thought that prison officers generally experienced difficulties in relating to ethnic minority prisoners. At Newfield and East Bridge Black inmates were almost invariably singled out as the focus of concern. The root of the problem was seen to emanate from the hostility which Black inmates displayed towards prison staff through their 'anti-authority attitudes', 'backchat', and 'lackadaisical manner'. Officers at Littlebourne were more evenly divided according to whether or not they fixed their attention upon Blacks, but amongst those who referred to relational difficulties with Black prisoners precisely the same sorts of reasons and explanations were put forward. Where they singled out Asian inmates, however, relational problems were linked with language difficulties and a lack of knowledge and understanding amongst prison staff rather than to the idiosyncracies of this particular racial group.

Racial stereotypes also came to the fore when 70 per cent of officers at Newfield, 60 per cent at East Bridge, and 40 per cent at Littlebourne claimed that the behaviour of Black inmates presented them with particular management problems.[3] In contrast, at all three establishments fewer than one in twenty thought that Whites, Asians, or any other racial group posed such problems. Most of the management problems which officers associated with Blacks centred on the ways in which they interacted with staff. Time and again negative stereotypes were employed to explain the difficulties which confronted staff in their dealings with these prisoners:

They're constantly winding the staff up with this arrogant attitude of theirs. The look that says 'I'll do it, but I'll do it in my own time'. (officer)

They stand around in their groups and when any of us walk by, they start swearing in their patois talk. They think we can't understand them so they'll get away with it. (officer)

---

[3] Over half of the officers interviewed at Wilding and Duxton endorsed this view.

Such depictions, however, would not appear to represent the kind of problems which might be expected to cause the greatest concern within the prison. Only at Newfield did prison officers suspect that Black inmates were at the centre of the most subversive activities. Elsewhere they were rarely mentioned as the main organizers of the smuggling activities, or of the bullying and extortion of other inmates. Nor were they seen as high escape risks or as the leaders of serious disturbances. These sorts of activities, particularly at Littlebourne, were acknowledged to be the domain of the White 'gangsters' or Irish 'terrorist' prisoners.

4. RACIAL STEREOTYPES AND INMATES' PROBLEMS

Many of the problems which the uniformed staff thought that prisoners generally experienced related to their lives outside the prison—such as the practical and emotional stresses associated with separation from their homes and families, and the frustration of being denied their freedom to go out 'on the town'. Other problems were seen to be specifically associated with their lives inside prison—such as lack of adequate facilities, relationships with other inmates, and relationships with prison staff. It is significant that as many as 82 per cent of the uniformed staff thought that the problems experienced by Black, White, and Asian inmates differed, either in nature or degree, on account of their racial origin. The most frequently cited problem for all racial groups was the experience of separation from wives, girlfriends, and children. Even so, fewer officers thought that Black or Asian inmates suffered because of this and, where they did, it was thought to be to a lesser degree.[4] They explained this by pointing to differences in the nature of family relationships, which they believed ethnic minority prisoners experienced. Black inmates, for example, were attributed with a 'macho image' and a greater sexual freedom, which staff associated with an 'easy come easy go' attitude towards wives and girlfriends. At the youth custody centre it was felt that

[4] 60% of officers cited this as a problem for Whites, but only 45% thought it was a problems for Black or Asian prisoners.

Black parents were more likely than their White counterparts to support and stand by their sons throughout their time in custody, thus causing these trainees less worry. The reasons why Asian inmates were thought to have fewer concerns about their outside relationships was that they could rely on the high level of support that was provided for their families by their close-knit communities.

But the greatest distinctions drawn by staff between the problems of White, Black, and Asian prisoners were in the ways in which they coped with life inside prison. The ordered regimes which govern prison life inevitably deny inmates choice over many aspects of daily living. Constraints are imposed upon what time they get out of bed, what time they take their meals, and when they may pursue their leisure activities. It is thus, perhaps, not surprising that one of the main hardships which prison officers thought all three racial groups experienced was their loss of autonomy, or freedom of action. This, however, was where the similarity ended.

Blacks and Asians were portrayed more often than White inmates as experiencing problems in relation to their lives inside the prison. Asians were seen as experiencing particularly acute problems in their relationships with other prisoners.[5] They were thought to be generally disliked by other racial groups and were frequently described as 'scapegoats', suffering from intimidation, bullying, and extortion. In addition, three out of ten officers thought that Asian prisoners suffered from a lack of adequate facilities within the prisons to meet their dietary customs and to enable them to practise their religions.

Once again, Black prisoners were looked upon in a completely different light. They were thought, far more often than Whites or Asians, to experience difficulties in their relationships with prison staff:[6]

The main problem that the Blacks have is the one they bring on themselves. It's their arrogant attitude . . . they're born with it . . . they won't accept authority . . . not from anyone. They think they're so big. (officer)

[5] 37% identified this as a problem for Asian prisoners, 24% mentioned it for Blacks, and 21% for Whites.

[6] 19% of officers mentioned this as a problem for Blacks, whereas 5% mentioned this for Whites, and 2% for Asians.

The thing about Blacks is that they're all anti-authority—the lot of them . . . they have this enormous chip on their shoulder. And that's what causes their problems in here. (officer)

It's that aggressive attitude of theirs . . . they won't do a damn thing when you tell them . . . they hang about in gaggles all over the place and when you try to move them on they get mouthy with you . . . (officer)

Officers described them as being generally disliked by prison staff because of their arrogant and anti-authority attitudes and, as a consequence, they were thought to be treated less generously than other inmates. There was no suggestion on the part of staff that Black inmates were being denied their rights. Rather, it was said that they suffered as a result of a more subtle process which denied them favours. Staff tended to go more 'by the book' with Black inmates and refused to bend the rules for them in ways which they often did for White inmates.

Thus it appeared that, in general, prison officers expressed sympathy for the trials and troubles suffered by Asian inmates, who were regarded to a large degree as victims in prison— unpopular amongst fellow inmates; subjected to ill-treatment and abuse; and culturally dispossessed. Black inmates, on the other hand, were accorded little sympathy. A constant refrain was that Black prisoners 'brought on their own problems' on account of their 'belligerent' and 'anti-authority' attitudes.

Given the range of problems which prison officers thought inmates experienced, it is not surprising that the majority felt that inmates needed some form of help in prison. There was, however, something of an anomaly here. Although eight out of ten officers distinguished between the problems suffered by White, Black, and Asian inmates, almost two-thirds thought that they required similar types of help. Those officers who did point to differences in the help required felt that Asian inmates needed less after-care or welfare because of the highly supportive nature of their families. Black inmates, on the other hand, were thought to need more of this sort of help because of the racial discrimination they faced in society and, especially amongst staff at Newfield, it was felt that Blacks needed assistance to improve their standards of education and training.

Virtually all the uniformed staff agreed that they had a central role to play in providing guidance and advice to prisoners. It was said that inmates of all races would call upon staff if this provided the ultimate solution to their problems. But over half of the officers thought that ethnic minority inmates were less likely than White prisoners to approach them and would do so only if absolutely necessary. The less frequent approaches made by Black and Asian prisoners were, however, explained in rather different ways. At all establishments Asian inmates were thought to require less assistance from staff because they acted as a self-supporting community in prison. At Littlebourne, in particular, it was said that Asian prisoners usually elected one spokesman who would liaise with officers on the problems of all Asian inmates on his wing:

Asians . . . tend to confide more in one another. They're a very close-knit community . . . they're less likely to talk to staff and may be a bit suspicious of them.

The Asians turn more to each other—they're very supportive and they usually all go through a spokesman who deals with all their problems.

On the other hand, about half of the officers at every prison thought that Black inmates were less likely to approach them because of their subversiveness, independence, and hostile stance towards prison officers:

They [Black prisoners] are more subversive and more secretive. Asians are less likely to come to us too but for different reasons. They feel more distant and more guarded. (officer)

Blacks can't show their weakness. (officer)

The Blacks tend to be more independent than the White boys. (officer)

It's a kind of inverse prejudice by Blacks. It comes down to social pressures—Blacks shouldn't even talk to White men, let alone White staff—there's nothing in common at all. (officer)

Blacks don't come to staff—it comes down to prejudice really—Black men don't want White staff knowing their problems. (officer)

5. RACIAL STEREOTYPING AMONGST OTHER STAFF

What has been presented so far concerns the perceptions of discipline staff who work mainly on the wing. It emerged, however, that their views were not wholly idiosyncratic. Officers who worked in the reception unit voiced exactly the same kinds of concerns, in similar forms of language, as other members of the uniformed staff. Officers and civilians responsible for the supervision of work parties were less likely than staff on the wings to single out particular racial groups as either presenting them with a management problem or as having any effect at all upon their day-to-day work. Nevertheless, where they did draw distinctions between racial groups the stereotypic line was closely followed. Over a third singled out the behaviour of Black prisoners as presenting them with particular problems. In addition to their 'backchat' and 'cliquishness' they were described by almost half of the work supervisors as being unwilling to work and by 34 per cent as producing bad workmanship, 'Negroes are miles behind. They don't want to work. They're naturally lazy and you can never get them to do it right when you do get them to work. They don't have the intelligence' (civilian work supervisor) White and Asian inmates were hardly ever mentioned in these terms. On the contrary, on the relatively few occasions when supervisors identified particularly good or willing workers, these tended to be Asian inmates.

Governors, probation officers, and education officers, however, hardly ever ascribed these kinds of pejorative differences to Black and Asian inmates. None of the governors singled out the behaviour of Black inmates as presenting them with particular management problems. Indeed, one went so far as to state, 'In real terms it's the Whites who are most subversive, although in terms of people's stereotypes staff would identify Blacks as creating the most disruption and being subversive. But this is simply not borne out in reality.' Probation officers did not find that ethnic minority inmates presented fundamentally different types of problems in prison, were especially demanding to deal with, or were any more or less likely to approach them for assistance. Education staff did not feel that ethnic minority prisoners presented particular behavioural problems in the classroom, or were any more or less enthusiastic than White inmates about their education.

An interesting finding was that, although members of the Boards of Visitors claimed that there were no differences in either the extent to which inmates of different racial origins approached them with petitions, or how frequently they appeared before them on adjudication, about a third of them thought that in any establishment a high proportion of Black prisoners led to increased disruption. They were, however, evenly divided about whether they thought this resulted from the innate 'hot-bloodedness' and 'belligerence' of Blacks, or from a misinterpretation by staff of culturally endorsed behaviour, 'What is taken for insolence in Blacks is not real insolence at all. It's just White perception of what is insolence.' (member of Board of Visitors)

6. THE DEFINITION OF RACE RELATIONS AS A PROBLEM OR AN ISSUE

The ways in which Black prisoners have been characterized and the effect their presence is seen to have upon the social organization of the prison suggests, at least to some extent, that race relations presents an exacting and difficult task for prison staff. Indeed, the finding that over half of the uniformed officers wanted to limit the numbers of Black prisoners in any single establishment strongly indicates that race relations is seen to be a feature of prison life which demands considerable regulation. In this context it might reasonably be expected that race relations would be defined as a problem by prison staff. But this was not the case. Although it was apparent that they closely associated the concept of race relations with the notion of a problem, they were at pains to point out that, in their view, it did not constitute a problem in prisons.

A common interpretation, and in fact criticism, made by staff about the Prison Department's race relations policy was that it assumed the existence of a race relations problem in prisons. With the exception of East Bridge, staff took every opportunity to declare that no such problem existed. This trend was confirmed when officers were questioned directly on the matter. Only at East Bridge did a majority of prison officers (66 per cent) think that race relations constituted a problem in their own establishment and for the prison system in general. In marked contrast, at Newfield and Littlebourne 80 per cent denied that any such problem existed.[7] This denial permeated all grades of

[7] At Wilding and Duxton 80% of uniformed staff denied the existence of a race relations problem in their own establishment.

the main staff groups working within the prisons, the only exceptions being probation officers, education staff, and psychologists. Indeed, five of the seven race relations liaison officers and eight of the twelve prison governors who were interviewed said that the state of race relations in their own establishment did not constitute a problem. Nor, in general, were any problems overtly referred to in the race relations liaison officers' annual reports. For the most part these focused upon the provision of facilities for ethnic minority inmates; the nature of contacts made with ethnic minority groups in the outside community; initiatives taken within individual establishments; and the generally harmonious nature of social relations amongst inmates.

Throughout the research many prison staff not only emphasized that race relations was not a problem but also rejected the notion that it was a relevant issue for the Prison Service. This was forcefully demonstrated in the response of many prison officers to our presence within their establishment. It was not uncommon for us to be asked why we were 'wasting our time' on such research or whether we had 'nothing better to do'. Considerable criticism was directed at the Prison Department for wasting time, effort, and money on developing a policy which was variously described as either addressing something which was not an issue or which succeeded only in creating an issue where none had previously existed:

Race relations is an issue as defined by politicians—not by me—it's never been an issue in my experience. It's the politicians who create a race mentality. (governor)

I don't even notice what colour they are . . . they're all treated the same in here. (officer)

It's the policies that create the problems. They highlight race. Before we had all these anti-discrimination Acts nobody noticed colour. (officer)

Among two-thirds of staff at East Bridge and the minority at the other establishments who felt that race relations was a problem for the Prison Service, the majority argued that the nature of the problem was rooted not in the prison but in the outside community, beyond their professional jurisdiction. In this respect prison was seen as a microcosm of society:

When you've got what you've got in Southall, what can you expect here? Of course it's a problem, but they've got to solve it out there first. (officer)

Well, it's just like in Brixton, isn't it? If they can't get on out there they're not going to become best mates in here, are they? (officer)

A lot of staff are racially prejudiced but they are a cross-section of society. Everyone is entitled to their own views. (officer)

Thus, they felt that there was little they could do within the Prison Service while racial problems existed outside. The fact that many more staff at East Bridge drew comparison with race relations in inner-city areas may explain why a much larger proportion than in the rurally sited prisons considered race relations to be a problem. In all prisons, however, there were a few officers who felt strongly that, regardless of race relations problems in society, the Prison Service had a duty to take firm action to counteract prejudice and discrimination within prisons. They decried the use of racist language; they abhorred the practice of racial stereotyping; and they demonstrated considerable concern about underlying racial tensions.

One reason why even those who identified race relations as a problem tended not to attach great significance to it was because racial tensions rarely resulted in violent physical confrontation and therefore were not seen to represent a threat to the good order of the establishment.[8] Furthermore, the majority of staff who did not perceive there to be a problem took the lack of overt racial conflict as positive proof of good race relations.

A consequence of this focus upon manifest racial conflict was that there was little recognition of the significance of racial tensions which existed at a latent and more subtle level. So entrenched was the tendency amongst prison staff to play down the relevance of race relations that, even when there was direct conflict between inmates of different races, the racal dimension was sometimes denied. Of course, not every disagreement between inmates of different races is rooted in racial conflict. Nevertheless during the period of field-work a number of altercations

---

[8] The fact that there had been a violent racial confrontation at East Bridge shortly before our visit may help to explain why more of the officers there defined race relations as a problem.

occurred, which, according to the participants, were motivated by racial hostility. Yet these incidents were interpreted by prison staff as having nothing to do with race relations. On one occasion, for example, a fight occurred between a group of White and a group of Black inmates, which resulted in one prisoner being seriously injured and another being transferred out of the prison. According to those inmates who had been involved, the fracas had been directly instigated by one of the White inmates who, while drunk on prison 'hooch', had been incited by two sober, self-declared, White racist prisoners to hurl racial abuse at the Blacks. Although those involved had explained this in their evidence, the situation was defined by staff as a struggle for power which was independent of any racial component. It was, therefore, deemed as irrelevant to concerns about race relations.

Prison governors and race relations liaison officers also gave examples of racial prejudice and discrimination, while, at the same time, denying that race relations were a problem:

I am manifestly aware of the racist views held by some of my colleagues. (governor)

Some prison officers deliberately stir up trouble by placing racist inmates to share cells with Blacks. (governor)

Black officers would need a lot of strength of personality to 'take stick' from every corner. (race relations liaison officer)

I know that they [other prison officers] call me 'Sambo-Samaritan'. (race relations liaison officer)

The fact that a majority of staff wanted to see the proportions of Black inmates within individual establishments strictly controlled, usually on the grounds that where the Black population reached a certain level problems inevitably broke out, casts further doubt upon their denial that race relations is a relevant issue for the Prison Service. Given this, the crucial question is why the significance of race remains unrecognized by prison staff, and, in particular, why they do not regard race relations as a problem.

Several factors contribute to this state of affairs, none of which should be deemed mutually exclusive. One important element is the pride which staff take in their work. All staff groups have a vested interest in playing down difficulties and presenting a good image, if only to maintain morale. This is not to suggest that the denial of any race relations problems represents a massive cover-up operation on the part of prison governors or the uniformed staff. On the contrary, it has more to do with the sets of priorities which operate in prison and the ways in which issues become identified as problems. The overriding concern with management and control has led prison staff to define as problems only those issues which represent an immediate threat to the smooth running of the establishment. An issue tended to be elevated to the status of a problem only if any of the following three criteria were met: first, the issue had to be manifestly apparent rather than latent or potentially problematic; second, it had to be specific to a particular establishment or, at least, specific to the prison system (situations which were seen to occur elsewhere were defined not as a 'problem' but as a 'fact of life'); third, an issue became a problem only if it could not be handled within the establishment.

There is, however, another process by which issues—whether identified as problems or not—are interpreted as pertinent to race relations. Indeed, as has already been mentioned, incidents of manifest conflict involving inmates of different races, although identified as problems, were not defined as being racial problems. A number of possible explanations may be advanced for this. For example, prison staff are prone to focus upon the immediate causes rather than upon the dynamics of conflict. This may preclude the recognition of a racial component in an incident, which, although not apparently motivated by racial prejudice or hostility, was escalated by underlying racial tensions.

What is certain is that the tendency for racial situations to remain unpublicized is enhanced by the propensity of prison officers to play down the significance of race relations in the daily round of prison life. One obvious contributing factor is the political sensitivity of race relations in the outside world. Some trepidation was expressed by officers that the introduction of a specific race relations policy in prison would 'create problems where none existed' and further damage the public image of the Prison Service by 'giving the popular press even more "dirt" on prison officers'. At the same time, however, the low profile attributed to race by prison staff is certainly not discouraged by the Prison Department's race relations policy statement, which uncompromisingly defines race relations as 'neither an extra burden nor a separable and discrete activity'.[9]

[9] Home Office (1983), Prison Department Circular Instruction 56/1983, para. 12.

4

Inmate Perspectives

The perception of social reality is inevitably shaped by the vantage points from which events are viewed. It is reasonable to expect that those at the bottom looking up see things differently from those at the top looking down. The discussion so far has focused upon the attitudes and beliefs held by prison staff about ethnic minority inmates. The purpose of this chapter is to examine the issue of race relations in prison from the perspective of the inmates.

The first section concerns the development of inmate social relations in prisons. Consideration is given to the ways in which race relations in prisons are influenced by the experience of imprisonment *per se* and by the identities which inmates bring with them from outside. The second section of the chapter examines in some detail the nature of the identities and pre-prison experiences of the three racial groups. It reveals the extent to which White, Black, and Asian inmates differ in terms of their socio-demographic profiles and pre-prison life-styles. Specific attention is paid to the question of how far the views and experiences of Black inmates substantiate staff depictions of them as alienated from the values associated with education and full-time employment, and with law and order. Thirdly, consideration is given to inmates' assessments of the state of race relations in prison; in particular, the extent to which they identify race relations as a problem, and their perceptions and experience of racial prejudice and discrimination. There will be some attempt to examine the degree to which the views of Black inmates conform to the racial stereotype held by prison officers. The fourth section focuses the discussion upon the extent and nature of racial grouping amongst inmates. It explores the ways in which the patterns of interaction which occur between different racial groups in prison are influenced by the nature of the inmate population, by the identities and social experiences which inmates bring with them into prison, and by the organizational and structural features of prison regimes.

1. PRISON LIFE, INMATE SOCIAL ORGANIZATION, AND RACE RELATIONS

Media reportage of prison overcrowding, roof-top protests, and other inmate disturbances has drawn the public's attention to some of the problems currently faced in the prison system. Such coverage, however, portrays little about the quality of life in prisons. The popular image of high Victorian walls, heavy gates, and barred windows within which Ronnie Barker 'Porridge' type characters spend their time in petty wheeling and dealing remains the nearest that most people ever get to the reality of prison life.

Only one of the three main prisons in the research, East Bridge, displayed the characteristically grim physical features of a Victorian heritage. On rainy days it appears shrouded in a steamy mist emitted by its ancient underground heating system. In keeping with most prisons of its vintage there is no integral sanitation and the degrading procedure of 'slopping out' occurs every morning. Within the prison there is little work and inmates' activities are strictly curtailed by the high degree of lock-up. Thus, in the main, contact with prisoners other than cellmates is limited to brief encounters in the meals queue and to periods of association in a large central hall, which occur once in every three evenings.

From a distance Littlebourne is more reminiscent of a modern age top-security communications installation. The high, pale walls surrounding the buildings are complemented by an inner security fence and high-powered mast lighting. Dogs are used to patrol the perimeter, whilst within the prison the doors are opened by remote control apparatus and inmates are relatively free to walk around unescorted, their movements monitored on a closed-circuit television system. The high priority accorded to work, education, and vocational training ensures that virtually all inmates are engaged in such activities for the greater part of the day. The men are allowed to associate freely every evening, during which time they may choose to watch television, play games, such as pool, darts, or cards, or pursue hobbies. As long-term prisoners they are permitted to buy and cook their own food and the aroma of roast chicken, peppered steaks or spicy curries frequently emanated from the small kitchenettes situated on the ground floor of each of the wings.

Newfield, on the other hand, with its somewhat sprawling and dilapidated buildings, cannot hide its previous identity in the 1940s as a prisoner of war camp. As at Littlebourne, trainees spend most of their day at work, in vocational training, or in education classes, and their evenings watching television or playing games, usually pool, with their friends. Unlike the two adult prisons, considerable emphasis is placed upon contact with the outside world. Most inmates, if they so choose, are able to work outside, tending the extensive prison grounds, and those who are deemed deserving are permitted to work within the local community.

A substantial body of academic literature now exists on the social organization of the prison. American research, in particular, has explored the ways in which inmates are socially organized in prisons and has questioned the origins of prisoner subculture. Two schools of thought have emerged within this literature. Some researchers view the inmate culture as emerging within the prison; others argue that it stems from the outside world. These two orientations have become known as the 'indigenous origin' model and the 'importation' model of inmate social organization.

The indigenous origin model suggests that prisoners collectively organize to overcome the deprivations associated with life in prison, so that an inmate culture emerges which is characterized by a normative code of solidarity.[1] Consequently, inmates are perceived as being socialized into a pre-existing cultural world, which is largely impermeable to influence from outside. The work of Gresham Sykes provides one of the

---

[1] G. M. Sykes (1958), *Society of Captives: A Study of a Maximum Security Prison* (Princeton, NJ: Princeton University Press); G. M. Sykes and S. M. Messinger (1960), 'The Inmate Social System', *Theoretical Studies in Social Organisation of the Prison*, Pamphlet No. 15 (New York: Social Science Research Council), 13–19; L. McCorkle and R. Korn (1954), 'Resocialisation within the Walls', *The Annals of the American Academy of Political and Social Science* (293, May), 88–98.

clearest examples of this approach.[2] In his study of the New Jersey State Maximum Security Prison he identified five major deprivations of imprisonment, which, he claims, facilitate a shared identity amongst inmates and structure their adaptations to prison life. These are: loss of liberty, loss of autonomy, loss of heterosexual activity, loss of privacy, and loss of possessions. Although only one of the three main establishments in this research is categorized as maximum security, it was clear that the same deprivations were felt by the sample of men who were interviewed. Regardless of racial origin and differences in prison regimes, the focal concerns of prisoners were markedly similar. The most frequently mentioned hardships were: missing their wives, girlfriends and families; the lack of freedom to go out drinking or to clubs; the lack of autonomy to resolve domestic problems; the restrictions placed upon their ability to structure their day; the boredom and monotony of the prison regime; and the enforced company of men with whom they would not choose to associate outside.

The importation model criticizes the concept of the prison as a closed system.[3] Proponents of this perspective argue that the ways in which prisoners adapt to imprisonment reflect pre-prison experiences. The inmate culture is thus depicted as being imported into the prison and as determined by factors outside the prison walls. Amongst the variables which have traditionally been considered to be important in this respect are socio-demographic factors, such as sexual identity, and socio-cultural factors, such as criminal orientation.[4] More recently American researchers have turned their attention to the impact of socio-political developments in the wider society. In particular, the politicization of Black people through the emergence of Black Muslim 'political' movements in the USA in the 1950s has been

[2] Sykes, *Society of Captives.*
[3] L. Carroll (1974), *Hacks, Blacks and Cons* (Lexington: Lexington Books, D. C. Heath and Co.); J. Irwin (1970), *The Felon* (Englewood Cliffs, NJ: Prentice Hall).
[4] R. Giallombardo (1966), *Society of Women: A Study of Women's Prisons* (New York: John Wiley and Sons); J. Irwin, and D. R. Cressey (1982), 'Thieves, Convicts and the Inmate Culture', *Social Problems*, 10: 142–55; D. Ward and G. Kassebaum (1965), *Women's Prison: Sex and Social Structure* (Chicago: Aldine).

deemed to be significant in explaining the racial cleavages found in American prisons:

The Black Muslims actively proselytised black prisoners preaching a doctrine of black superiority. They imported the spirit of 'black nationalism' into the prisons, catalysed the frustration and bitterness of black prisoners, and provided organisational and ideological tools for challenging the authority of white prison officials . . . In any case, the modern 'crisis in corrections' is attributable to the changing pattern of race relations which began with the Muslim protests.[5]

The relevance of the importation model for race relations in British prisons has already been demonstrated in the previous chapters. Implicit in officers' assessments of the state of race relations in prisons is the notion that ethnic minority inmates enter prison with distinct racial and cultural identities, and that these are highly influential in shaping their adaptations to prison life.

At one time the indigenous origin and importation models were presented as being contradictory. This polarization, however, has recently been considered to be unnecessary and even misleading.[6] It is now seen as imperative that the analysis of inmate social organization and patterns of race relations in prison take account both of the unique characteristics of the prisons and the culture and social structure of the wider society.

2. THE INFLUENCE OF THE 'OUT'

(i) A Socio-Demographic Profile

This research examined the extent to which White, Black, and Asian prisoners present different socio-demographic profiles in terms of age, country of birth, marital status, family circumstances, and childhood history. Since ethnic monitoring is a relatively recent development in prisons, it is perhaps not surprising that little information exists on a national scale about

---

[5] J. B. Jacobs (1979), 'Race Relations and the Prisoner Subculture', in N. Morris and M. Tonry, (eds.), *Crime and Justice: An Annual Review of Research* (Chicago: University of Chicago Press), 1–27.

[6] Carroll, *Hacks, Blacks and Cons.* Jacobs, 'Race Relations and the Prisoner Subculture'.

the ethnic minority prison population. The most recent statistics merely classify ethnic minority prisoners by age, sex, offence group, and type of prisoner.[7]

With regard to age, the *Prison Statistics* only categorize ethnic minority inmates as young offenders (aged under 21), or adult prisoners (aged over 21). According to these data young offenders constituted approximately 1 in 4 of the White and Black populations under sentence on 30 June 1986 and 1 in 6 of the Asians. The interview sample closely mirrored this national picture, with young offenders accounting for 29 per cent of the White, 32 per cent of the Black and 25 per cent of the Asian respondents. An important common denominator amongst the young offenders was that virtually all of them, regardless of race, had been born in Britain.

The official statistics provide no information about the age distribution of the adult ethnic minority prison populations. However, demographic data gathered from interviews and prisoner records suggest that significant differences exist in both the age structure and national background of White, Black, and Asian adult prisoners. Analysis of the sample of Standard Classification Forms, completed for a total of 1255 adult prisoners, revealed that a signficantly higher proportion of Black (64 per cent) than of White (41 per cent) and Asian inmates (38 per cent) were aged under thirty.[9] In addition to being younger it also emerged that Black adult prisoners were more likely than Asians to have been born in Britain. Almost half of the Black inmates for whom records were consulted were British-born, compared with only one in ten of the Asians.

These differences were also clearly in evidence amongst the interview sample. The paucity of older Black prisoners at both East Bridge and Littlebourne severely restricted the population from which interviewees could be drawn. In consequence, the

[7] 'Type of prisoner' refers to the status of the prisoner, i.e. untried prisoners, convicted unsentenced prisoners, sentenced prisoners; and/or type of sentence, i.e. detention centre, youth custody, adult prison up to 18 months, adult prison over 18 months.

[8] Home Office (1987), *Prison Statistics, England and Wales 1986*, Cm. 210 (London: HMSO), 32, table 1.12.

[9] These forms were completed for prisoners serving sentences of 18 months and above, and were drawn from 8 prisons in the South-East and Midlands regions. See ch. 1. $\chi^2 = 63.03$; $df = 2$; $p < 0.01$.

sample of Black prisoners included a considerable over-representation of men in the younger age-groups. Approximately half of the White (51 per cent) and Asian (47 per cent) adult respondents but over three-quarters of the Blacks (79 per cent) were aged under 30. It is also salient that half (53 per cent) of the Black sample had been born in Britain and virtually all of those born in the West Indies had emigrated to Britain before they had reached the age of 18. In striking contrast all of the Asian interviewees had been born in India, Pakistan, or Bangladesh, and most of them had entered Britain as adults.

The clear inference of the research is that, in the South-East prison region at least, important distinctions exist in the age profile and national background of adult Black and Asian prisoners sentenced to medium and long terms of imprisonment. Black inmates, as a group, tend to be younger than either Whites or Asians, and to be drawn from that sector of society known as second generation Blacks. In other words, they are the offspring of Black immigrants who settled in Britain in the 1950s and 1960s. Asian prisoners, on the other hand, tend to be older and to be either first generation immigrants or foreign nationals.

Not unexpectedly, given the differential age distribution, significant differences were also found in relation to the marital status, family structures, and domestic circumstances of the three racial groups. The data gathered from Standard Classification Forms revealed that a much higher proportion of Asian prisoners (72 per cent) than either Whites or Blacks were married.[10] Almost all of the remaining Asians were single. White inmates, on the other hand, were equally as likely to be married (32 per cent) as single (33 per cent), and had the highest divorce rate (18 per cent) of the three racial groups. In sharp contrast, very few Black inmates were married (13 per cent).[11] Black prisoners tended to describe themselves as either single (42 per cent) or cohabiting with a common law wife (38 per cent).

The same patterns were reflected amongst the interview sample, although owing to the inclusion of youth custody

[10] $\chi^2 = 73.08$ $df = 3$ $p < 0.01$.

[11] $\chi^2 = 78.66$ $df = 3$ $p < 0.01$. Even when only those inmates aged under 30 were considered, Blacks were significantly more likely than Whites to be cohabiting rather than married. $\chi^2 = 41.34$ $df = 3$ $p < 0.01$.

trainees a greater number of all racial groups described themselves as single. None the less, despite differences in age and marital status, approximately half of all the men interviewed, regardless of race, had children. But whereas almost all of the Asian fathers had been living with their children immediately before their imprisonment, this was the case for fewer than half of the Whites (48 per cent) and only a third of the Blacks (32 per cent).

These racial differences were not limited to the men's current family ties and domestic arrangements but were reflected to some extent in their own childhood experiences. Virtually all of the Asian prisoners who were interviewed, and the overwhelming majority (81 per cent) for whom Standard Classification Forms had been completed, were reared by both of their parents, whereas this was so for only half of the White and Black inmates. Amongst the remainder, most of the Blacks had been brought up by a consistent single parent, usually their mother, while the Whites tended to have oscillated from one parent to another and to have spent time in children's homes or foster care.

(ii) Alienated Minorities? Work, Education, and Training

It will be recalled that prison officers commonly perceived both Black and Asian prisoners as being alienated from British society. Black prisoners were typically described as hostile to authority and as rejecting the values associated with law and order, hard work, and deferred gratification. The fact that it had proved so difficult to encourage their recruitment to the Prison Service was used as evidence of the estrangement felt by Black people towards the society in which they lived. They were perceived as unwilling to work and as less able than any other racial group to compete in the job market. The lack of ability ascribed to them was explained both by reference to poor educational standards and to a rebellious attitude towards authority.

Asian prisoners, on the other hand, were depicted as being alienated from British society not because they were hostile to established authority or to the values of achievement through hard work and industry, but because they distanced themselves by maintaining distinct cultural life-styles imported from their countries of origin. It was believed that Asian people did not join the Prison Service because it was outside their well-established routes of mobility, such as accountancy, shopkeeping, and the textile industries.

To test the strength of these generalizations, information was gathered about the employment and educational histories of adult prisoners from the sample of Standard Classification Forms.[12] The majority (78 per cent) of these inmates, regardless of race, described themselves as either 'unskilled workers' (34 per cent), or as 'skilled or semi-skilled' (44 per cent). Very few (2 per cent) had never worked and most of these were younger prisoners aged between 21 and 24.

However, important differences emerged in the duration for which inmates had held their jobs. The most important factor to influence how long an inmate had been employed in any particular job was that of age. Amongst the sample as a whole, inmates aged over 30 were almost twice as likely as those under 30 to have held the same job for more than three years. Within these age-bands, however, clear racial differences emerged. Asians, regardless of their age, tended to have had more stable work records than either Whites or Blacks. Of the 100 Asians for whom information was available 85 per cent of the over thirties and 43 per cent of those in their twenties had held the same job for more than three years. There was little difference in the work records of the older White and Black inmates, amongst whom approximately two-thirds had worked for the same employer for at least three years. But amongst the younger age-group over a third (38 per cent) of the White inmates but only a quarter of the Blacks had held a job for this length of time.[13]

A similar pattern emerged when the employment histories of interviewees were examined. A higher proportion (28 per cent) of the interview sample was chronically unemployed, but this was relatively evenly spread across racial groups and tended to be concentrated amongst the younger inmates. Most (68 per cent) of the sample had intermittent employment histories— namely short-term, unskilled work interspersed with periods of

---

[12] See ch. 1.   [13] $\chi^2 = 4.11$ $df = 1$ $p < 0.05$.

unemployment. Again racial differences were most pronounced in the distribution of inmates who had been in continuous employment. Fewer than one in ten Black prisoners had a continuous work record compared with one in three Whites.

The lower incidence of stable employment records amongst the younger Black inmates is perhaps not surprising when account is taken, first, of the rise in unemployment in Britain over the last eight years; and second, of the findings of the latest Policy Studies Institute (PSI) survey, which showed that Black males suffer almost double the rate of unemployment found amongst White males because of the greater vulnerability of the lower level occupations in which they tend to work.[14]

There was little evidence to support the stereotype that Black inmates are alienated from education and vocational training. Information drawn from the sample of Standard Classification Forms showed that Black prisoners did not lack motivation to attend education and training courses. Although the majority of all races had left school at the minimum age, Black prisoners, irrespective of age, were significantly more likely than Whites to have taken courses in further education outside prison and to have attended education classes in prison.[15] A similar picture emerged with regard to vocational training. Blacks, and especially those in the younger age groups who had been born in the UK, demonstrated a significantly greater commitment than either White or Asian inmates. Altogether, 48 per cent of Blacks began some form of vocational training and almost half of these succeeded in completing it; whereas 38 per cent of Whites began a course and only 40 per cent managed to complete it.[16] It was the Asian prisoners whose records showed the least commitment to vocational training. Whilst similar numbers of

[14] C. Brown (1984), *Black and White Britain: The Third PSI Survey*, Policy Studies Institute (London: Heinemann), 151–4.

[15] 32% of Black inmates but only 17% of Whites had received further education outside prison; $\chi^2 = 29.72$ $df = 2$ $p < 0.01$. This significance remained even when only those inmates aged under 30 were considered. 55% of Blacks and 43% of Whites had attended education classes inside prison. $\chi^2 = 6.26$ $df = 1$ $p < 0.05$. Differences remained even when only those inmates aged under 30 were considered. The figures for Asian inmates were 34% and 36%, respectively.

[16] $\chi^2 = 6.85$ $df = 2$ $p < 0.05$. Differences remained even when only those inmates aged under 30 were considered.

Asians as Whites had embarked upon a training course, only a quarter of them had seen it through to the end.[17]

Thus, it seems that far from being alienated from the values of educational achievement Black prisoners demonstrated a commitment which exceeded that of the Whites. This was further reflected in the interviews, where it emerged that Blacks were not only more likely than Whites to have taken further education courses outside prison but were also more likely than Whites to feel that they had benefited from the education classes they had attended in prison. Only 13 per cent of the Blacks expressed any negative views about the courses, compared with 30 per cent of the Whites. Moreover, a higher proportion of Black than White respondents had qualifications beyond CSE examinations. It is, perhaps, also worth pointing to the findings of the PSI study concerning education and training in the wider community. The survey, amongst men in the 16 to 24 age-group, noted that the proportion of Blacks gaining an apprenticeship or City and Guilds qualification is increasing and is now very close to that of Whites.[18]

(iii) Alienated Minorities? Crime, the Police, and the Courts

When prison officers referred to the anti-authority attitudes of Black inmates they typically alluded to their alienation from the criminal justice system and their hostility towards prison staff. Whilst Asian inmates were characterized as 'one-off' offenders, who generally demonstrated a commitment to the institutions of law and order, Black prisoners were portrayed as committing crime as part of their way of life and as displaying a general antipathy to the police, the courts, and the prisons. Yet the data drawn from interviews with inmates, from an analysis of the sample of Standard Classification Forms, and from published Home Office statistics fail to substantiate this stereotypic image of the Black prison population.

[17] These data do not reveal the nature of the education courses or vocational training engaged in by the inmates. There are, of course, important differences in starting and completing a four-year apprenticeship in mechanical engineering and six months training in catering under a Youth Opportunities Programme.   [18] Brown, *Black and White Britain*, pp. 134–5.

The charge that Black prisoners are more heavily involved in crime was not corroborated by Home Office statistics published in June 1986. Instead the data showed that White prisoners had substantially more previous convictions than Blacks. For adult men received under sentence into prison establishments in the period 1 July 1984 to 31 March 1985, 62 per cent of Whites had six or more previous convictions, compared with 48 per cent of Blacks, and 20 per cent of Asians.[19] These differences become more pronounced when the proportion of prisoners with eleven or more previous convictions is examined: 38 per cent of White receptions fell into this category, compared with 22 per cent of Black, and 8 per cent of Asians. Even where the nature of the offence was taken into account similar patterns emerged.

The previous criminal histories of the interview sample and of prisoners whose Standard Classification Forms were consulted closely resembled this national picture. It could, of course, be argued that the reason why Blacks have fewer previous convictions than Whites is that they are younger. This did not, however, prove to be the case. Significant differences remained even when only the Standard Classification Forms of those inmates who were aged under 30 were considered. Whilst the overwhelming majority of both Whites (94 per cent) and Blacks (95 per cent) entered prison with previous convictions, Whites were significantly more likely than Blacks to have had more. A third of the Whites but only a quarter of the Blacks entered prison with eleven or more previous convictions to their name.[20] Nor was there any evidence from the interviews that Black inmates started their criminal careers at an earlier age than did Whites. The vast majority of both White and Black prisoners received their first conviction before they reached the age of 21.

Yet despite being younger and having fewer previous convictions, Black inmates were as likely as Whites to have served previous sentences of imprisonment. Three-quarters of the White and Black inmates for whom Standard Classification Forms were completed and two-thirds of those who were

---

[19] Home Office (1986), *The Ethnic Origin of Prisoners: The Prison Population on 30th June 1985 and Persons Received, July 1984—March 1985.* (Statistical Bulletin, 17/86), 35, table 13.   [20] $\chi^2 = 5.5$ $df = 1$ $p < 0.05$.

interviewed had been in prison before. In striking contrast, fewer than a third of the Asian inmates had experienced previous custodial sentences.[21]

Fludger found a similar pattern amongst Blacks and Whites in his study of borstal trainees, and concluded that Black trainees were receiving custodial sentences at an earlier stage in their criminal careers than were Whites. He attributed these discrepancies, at least in part, to a higher rate of violent offending amongst Black trainees.[22] In his analysis of the current and previous convictions of borstal boys he found that Blacks were over-represented amongst those convicted of offences involving injury, assault, affray, robbery, rape, and indecent assault, and under-represented amongst those convicted of property offences, such as arson, criminal damage, burglary, theft, and car theft.

It is perhaps noteworthy that in Fludger's study the experience of Asian borstal trainees was seen to resemble closely that of Blacks. Unfortunately the available Home Office statistics provide no information concerning the nature of the previous convictions of ethnic minority inmates. Nor was it feasible to replicate Fludger's analysis in this research.

Important differences, however, were found in the nature of the current convictions of White, Black, and Asian inmates. Published Home Office statistics for the population under sentence in prison and youth custody establishments on 30 June 1986 show no major differences in the proportions of White, Black and Asian inmates convicted of first order offences of violence against the person or rape.[23] But they do indicate a greater propensity for Black youth custody trainees and adult prisoners to have been convicted of offences of robbery. As many as a quarter of Black youth custody trainees were serving sentences for robbery, compared with fewer than one in ten of the White trainees, and one in six of the Asians. This was

---

[21] $\chi^2 = 93.50$ $df = 1$ $p < 0.01$.

[22] N. Fludger (1981), *Ethnic Minorities in Borstal* (London: Home Office, Prison Department, Directorate of Psychological Services), 21; Fludger also found a high incidence of violent offending amongst Asian borstal trainees. However, this was not evident in this research.

[23] Home Office, *Prison Statistics England and Wales 1986*, p. 32, table 1.12.

balanced by a lower rate of convictions for burglary amongst young Blacks. Only a quarter of the Black youth custody trainees had been convicted of such offences, as opposed to more than a third of the Whites. A similar inverse relationship between robbery and burglary offences was noted amongst White and Black adult prisoners. Asian adults, however, presented a completely different offence profile from any other group. A striking 41 per cent of the Asian adult prison population had been convicted of drugs offences, compared with fewer than one in six of any other racial group. These differences in the offence profiles of White, Black, and Asian prisoners were clearly reflected in the data drawn from the sample of Standard Classification Forms and from inmate interviews.

Obviously the chances of anyone receiving a prison sentence are influenced by decisions taken at earlier stages of the criminal justice process. If, for example, Black people are more likely to be stopped, searched, arrested, and charged by the police, then it follows that they are going to appear in court earlier and more often than Whites. An overview of research on the subject of Black people and the police has recently been well documented by Iain Crow.[24] He presents an accumulation of evidence testifying to the troubled nature of relationships between the police and Black people. In 1981 Lord Scarman commented on the part played by the police and the Black community in the Brixton disorders:

the police must carry some responsibility for the outbreak of disorder. First, they were partly to blame for the breakdown in community relations. Secondly, there were instances of harassment and racial prejudice among junior officers on the streets of Brixton which gave credibility and substance to the arguments of the police's critics. Thirdly, there was the failure to adjust policies and methods to meet the needs of policing a multi-racial society. . . . The community and community leaders in particular must take their share of the blame for the atmosphere of distrust and mutual suspicion between the police and the community.[25]

[24] I. Crow (1987), 'Black People and Criminal Justice in the U.K.', *The Howard Journal of Criminal Justice* 26/4 (Nov.), 304–7.

[25] The Rt. Hon. Lord Scarman, OBE (1981), *The Scarman Report: The Brixton Disorders 10–12 April 1981* (London: Penguin), 118–19.

Since then a growing body of research has shown that young Blacks are disproportionately more likely than Whites to be the subject of police stop and search powers; that they are less likely than Whites to be cautioned and more likely to be arrested and prosecuted; and that racial prejudice plays some part in this process.[26]

It has been suggested that such practices have a negative impact upon the attitudes of Black people towards the police. A study by Gaskell published in 1986 found that young Blacks expressed more negative attitudes to the police than did young Whites, not because the police were seen as symbols of an oppressive White society but because of the nature of policing strategies.[27]

In a similar vein, this research largely confirmed the portrayal of Black prisoners as critical of the police, but the stereotype of them as indiscriminately antipathetic to the police was not borne out. Interviews conducted in the three main establishments revealed that Black prisoners had experienced greater levels of discordant contact with the police and were more critical than Whites on these grounds. About two-thirds of White and Black inmates had, at some time, been arrested by the police but eventually released without being charged: over 80 per cent of both groups claimed that this had happened to them on more than one occasion. Black prisoners, however, were considerably more likely than Whites to report that they had been stopped and questioned by the police, and to have experienced this more frequently. Almost 90 per cent of Black inmates said that they had been stopped and questioned in the street and half (53 per cent) claimed that this had occurred on six or more occasions. In comparison, 70 per cent of White inmates said that they had been stopped in this way and fewer than a third (29 per cent) had experienced this more than six times.

[26] C. Willis (1983), *The Use, Effectiveness and Impact of Police Stop and Search Powers*, Research and Planning Unit Paper No. 15 (London: HMSO); D. J. Smith and J. Gray (1983), *Police and People in London, IV: The Police in Action*, (London: Policy Studies Institute); S. F. Landau (1981), 'Juveniles and the Police', *British Journal of Criminology*, 21: 27–46; S. F. Landau and G. Nathan (1983), 'Selecting Delinquents for Cautioning in the London Metropolitan Area', *British Journal of Criminology*, 23: 28–49.
[27] G. Gaskell (1986), 'Black Youth and the Police', *Policing*, 2 (1), 26–34.

These differences were mirrored in inmates' assessments of police behaviour and in the extent to which they had called upon the police as 'consumers' of their services. When asked about the treatment they had received from police officers half of the White inmates but nearly two-thirds of the Blacks felt that they had been unfairly treated. The sort of complaints which Blacks and Whites made, however, were strikingly similar, tending to focus upon physical attacks, dishonesty, and unscrupulousness:

The police just abuse their power. They burst into my house and wrecked it . . . at the station I wouldn't answer their questions and so these two CID officers got hold of my head by my ears and smashed it against the counter . . . I wanted to make a complaint but my solicitor told me to forget it. (White, East Bridge)

They pull you in for no reason—just to give you a hard time. In my area it happens all the time. They leave you in the cells for hours and then start questioning you about all these different crimes. They try and kid you along that they know it was you. They say things like, 'we know you done it because we've got your prints', or 'so and so saw you leaving'. And you know it's a lie. Or they'll say they will drop charges on this if you say you did something else. There was this one time when they said I'd pulled a knife on someone and that they'd got the knife. They said they knew it was mine. But it wasn't mine and in the end it wasn't my fingerprints. (Black, Newfield)

They fitted me up on this charge by threatening to charge my wife with a whole string of offences that she is totally innocent of. The fact is the police in —— are bent. They manufacture evidence and there's fuck all you can do about it. (White, Littlebourne)

Very few of the inmates, however, applied these criticisms to all of their dealings with the police. Sometimes they provided accounts of good conduct:

The police in —— are real bastards and they'll set you up for anything. They've done it to me loads of times. But some police are OK, like those in —— . They treat you properly and you can have a chat and a laugh with them. (Black, Littlebourne)

I've been set up by the police and picked up by them for nothing. But most of them are OK and a lot do go by the book. It's only a few of them who are heavy and really have it in for you. (Black, Newfield)

Amongst the prisoners who were interviewed during this research almost all of the Blacks (93 per cent) and the majority of Whites (71 per cent) thought that the police were racially prejudiced. Moreover, eight out of ten of the Blacks and half of the Whites maintained that their assertions were based upon first-hand experience:

I've been arrested with Black lads before and I've seen with my own eyes how they get treated. They definitely get a worse deal. I was arrested this time with one Black and one White friend. Me and the White lad were allowed to keep our clothes but my Black friend was stripped and just had a blanket. (White, Littlebourne)

The police came and searched the house. They grabbed hold of me and pushed me up against the wall. One policeman asked me if I could breathe. I said 'No'. He said 'Good. Die you Black bastard'. (Black, Littlebourne)

But again, very few inmates asserted that this prejudice was pervasive throughout the police. For the most part, racial prejudice was thought to be either contained within certain sections of the police or restricted to a certain proportion of them:

Some police are OK, especially the older ones who are more understanding. With the younger ones the job goes to their head, you get a lot of rudeness out of them . . . I think for a lot of them they feel victimised by Black people—perhaps it all started at school and subconsciously they want to get back. (Black, Newfield)

Some are prejudiced and they don't think that Black people should be in their country. It comes out in the way they talk to you. I've been called a Black bastard and told to get back on my banana boat and go home. But they're not all like that—prejudiced, I mean. I suppose it's about fifty-fifty. (Black, East Bridge)

The mistrust which inmates, and in particular Black prisoners, expressed toward the police was reflected in their reluctance to seek assistance when they were themselves the victims of crime. Approximately a quarter of the inmates interviewed said that they had been a victim of a violent crime. Yet the majority of both Whites (68 per cent) and Blacks (75 per cent) who had experienced such an attack did not report it to the police. A larger proportion (40 per cent) of both Black and White inmates had been a victim of a property crime. But in this case 70 per cent of Blacks did not report the event to the police, whereas 70 per cent of Whites did. When inmates were asked to explain why they had failed to notify the police, the responses of Whites and Blacks were remarkably similar—more than two-thirds of them expressed a lack of confidence in and hostility to the police:

I don't think they'd take it seriously. They'd see it as a big joke. Tit for tat. (Black victim of theft)

Why would I report it to the police? They wouldn't do anything about it other than use it as an opportunity to poke their noses into my business. (White victim of assault)

I don't trust them and I want nothing to do with them, I'd rather sort it out myself. (Black victim of burglary)

Dissatisfaction with the courts was also high amongst inmates, particularly amongst the Blacks. A substantial minority of White prisoners (43 per cent) but nearly three-quarters of the Blacks (72 per cent) thought that the courts were racially prejudiced. Moreover, over half the Black inmates (58 per cent) claimed that they had first-hand experience of this. Amongst all prisoners it was widely believed that racial prejudice was more prevalent in the magistrates' courts than in the Crown Court. This was because the magistrates' courts were thought to have a close relationship with the police. Prejudice in the courts was said to be displayed in many ways:

It's a lot more difficult for Black people to get bail. Just look at C wing. I think it's because they think Black people do a lot of crimes and they want us off the streets. (Black, East Bridge)

It works to the disadvantage of foreigners. Solicitors and barristers just don't bother and it's impossible for foreigners to understand what is going on. (Cypriot, Littlebourne)

In my case—yes. I definitely got a longer sentence than if I'd been White because the court saw me as a Black man attacking a White woman. (Black, Littlebourne)

The courts don't want to be seen as racially prejudiced, so they give the coloureds an easier ride. In my view that's prejudice the other way round. (White, Newfield)

Despite the clear dissatisfaction which Black prisoners expressed about the operation of policing and court processes, there was no evidence to suggest that they were particularly hostile to the fact of their imprisonment. When asked about the justice of their own sentences, approximately two-thirds of both White

(69 per cent) and Black (65 per cent) prisoners considered that they had deserved a prison sentence for the offences they had committed. Furthermore, only one in five of the Blacks and one in four of the Whites thought that their sentence was too long. Thus the evident distinction between Black inmates' experiences of and attitudes towards the police, and their general acceptance of the justice of their own sentences throws into question the simplicity of the stereotypic image of Black prisoners as hostile to law and order. Their discordant experiences with the police and the selective way in which they criticized the police and the courts may be seen to represent more a concern with the means by which justice is achieved than a general antipathy towards the aims of the criminal justice system *per se.*

The experiences and attitudes of the small number of Asian prisoners were in marked contrast to those of the Blacks. Indeed, they were largely concordant with the stereotypes which officers held about them. Interviews conducted with inmates during the course of the research indicated that Asian prisoners stood apart from Whites and Blacks in terms of the extent and the nature of their contacts with the police. For Asian prisoners discordant experiences with the police were relatively rare: only three (18 per cent) had been arrested hv the police and eventually released without being charged, and only seven (41 per cent) had been stopped and questioned by the police. In addition, they were more likely than either Whites or Blacks to have sought help from the police when they were the victims of crime. Indeed, four out of the five who said they had been the victims of property offences and two of the three who said that they had sufferent violent assaults stated that they had reported it to the police. Given the very different nature of their contacts with the police, it is perhaps not surprising that Asian prisoners did not reflect the same sense of distrust and dissatisfaction as either the Whites or Blacks. Nine of them (53 per cent) considered that they had been fairly and even-handedly dealt with by the police. Only seven (41 per cent) thought that the police were racially prejudiced and just four (23 per cent) thought that such prejudice was evident in the courts. Paradoxically the Asians who had voiced so little criticism of the police or the courts were those who protested most about the injustice of their sentences: virtually all (82 per cent) of them felt that they had not deserved to go to prison at all.

(iv) A Question of Racial Identity

In striking contrast to the American experience, this study found no evidence of organized political activity amongst Black prisoners. Contact with inmates who were members of political and terrorist organizations outside prison appeared to have had no impact upon the political consciousness of Black prisoners. The levels of hostility and segregation between Whites and Blacks reported in Carroll's study of a maximum security prison in the USA were similarly absent amongst the inmates in the five prisons and youth custody centres studied here.[28]

None the less, it would be misleading to suggest that Black and Asian inmates lacked any group identity and that this was not rooted within a perception of Black and Asian people as economically, politically, and socially discriminated against in the wider society. A plethora of evidence testifies to the relative disadvantage suffered by ethnic minority groups in various spheres of social life. Black and Asian people have traditionally experienced higher levels of unemployment than Whites and have tended to be employed in low-status, low-income sectors of the labour market.[29] The third PSI survey published in 1984 concludes that the tenacity of the disadvantage experienced by ethnic minorities in the field of employment is due to a number of factors, in particular, to different educational backgrounds of workers in different ethnic groups; the lack of fluency in English amongst Asian workers; different residential locations of Black, Asian, and White workers; and direct and indirect racial discrimination.[30] Although reported instances of direct discrimination are less common than they used to be, differences are still to be found in the housing conditions of different ethnic groups.[31] In education, too, concern has been felt about the lack

---

[28] Carroll, *Hacks, Blacks and Cons*, pp. 39–42, 147–71, 182–90, 194–5, 206–7.

[29] Brown *Black and White Britain*, p. 293; A. Barber (1985), 'Ethnic Origin and Economic Status', *Employment Gazette*, 93: 467–77.

[30] Brown, *Black and White Britain*, pp. 150–84.   [31] Ibid. 68–95.

of proper attention paid by the system to the needs of ethnic minority children.[32] Moreover, the uneasy relationship between Black people and the police provides a potentially strong reinforcement of their racial identity; while for Asians there are the additional factors of language and religion which contribute to separate subcultural identities within the wider racial group.

To some extent, however, the strength of the separate racial identities possessed by the Black and Asian prisoners who took part in this research was mediated by their outside contacts with White people. Over 90 per cent of Black prisoners interviewed and most of the Asians said that outside prison they had White friends. The close relationships which Black prisoners, in particular, had with members of White society, especially their family ties with White women and their criminal links with White co-defendants, facilitated an awareness of shared problems and, to some degree, a common position in society. Indeed, the majority of White, Black, and Asian inmates said that they had friends of different races outside prison, although social contact between Blacks and Asians seemed to be relatively limited.

3. VIEWS OF RACE RELATIONS IN PRISONS

(i) Race Relations as a Problem: Racial Prejudice and Racial Dominance

When prisoners were asked whether they thought that race relations constituted a problem in their establishment, their replies were complex and conditional, and did not reflect the homogeneity of response found amongst prison officers. Of particular significance were the differences in the responses of inmates of different racial origins. Throughout their assessments Asian inmates were less likely than either Whites or Blacks to define race relations as being in any way problematic in prisons.

---

[32] A. Little (1975), 'The Educational Achievement of Ethnic Minority Children in London Schools', in G. Verma and C. Bagley (eds.), *Race and Education Across Cultures* (London: Heinemann); 48–69. Committee of Inquiry into the Education of Children from Ethnic Minority Groups (1981), *West Indian Children in our Schools* (London: HMSO).

Whilst the small number of Asian inmates who were interviewed precluded testing the statistical signficance of these differences, they were nevertheless consistent and all in the same direction.

Although half (52 per cent) of all racial groups thought that race relations constituted a problem in the wider prison system, the majority (64 per cent) denied that this was a problem in their own establishment. Asians were least likely to perceive race relations as a problem in their present establishment and White prisoners were the most likely.[33] Every inmate who thought that race relations was a problem identified human relationships as the focus for concern rather than the lack of special facilities. But the type of human relationships mentioned varied between the different races, with Black inmates (31 per cent) being twice as likely as Whites (14 per cent) to express concern about interaction between inmates and staff. For their part, White inmates tended to describe the problem in terms of social relations amongst the inmate population.

Inmates' attitudes towards the provision of special facilities for ethnic minorities within the prison were consistently favourable and did not reflect the resentment and jealousy which many prison staff had anticipated.[34] Indeed, the overwhelming majority of prisoners in all establishments approved of: the services of visiting priests from different religions (96 per cent); catering for a range of diets (94 per cent); supplying ethnic minority newspapers (87 per cent); and adapting the canteen supplies to meet the needs of ethnic minorities (91 per cent). There was also a high degree of support for facilities which could be interpreted as offering ethnic minorities preferential treatment, such as permission to have time off work to celebrate religious feasts (78 per cent) and to be allowed specially prepared foods during religious festivals (83 per cent) while continuing to be allowed to participate in the Christian festivities at Christmas. In addition almost two-thirds (64 per cent) felt that ethnic minority inmates should be offered education classes taught in their own languages. Only 6 per cent identified any disadvantages in providing any of these facilities.

Overall there was a high degree of satisfaction with the range

[33] Only three (18%) Asians identified the issue as problematic, compared with 35% of Blacks, and 41% of Whites.   [34] See ch. 2.

of facilities currently provided in the establishments, although a higher proportion of Blacks (50 per cent) and Asians (35 per cent) than Whites (17 per cent) thought that too little attention had been paid to their provision. These inmates were not, however, always discontented about facilities which related to their own ethnic groups. Black prisoners, for example, expressed concern about the services provided for Asian prisoners. Although the criticisms were very wide ranging, they tended to focus upon the inadequacies of existing services or arrangements rather than their total absence. Complaints were voiced most frequently about the quality and quantity of food available on the special diets; the lack of facilities enabling prisoners not normally resident in this country to maintain contact with their families; and the lack of opportunities for inmates to practise their religions:

Muslims in general suffer, because the vegetarian diet is so bad here. They just don't understand how to make vegetable dishes nutritious and filling. What happens is that we all fill up on potatoes. (Black, East Bridge)

My letters have to be translated so that they can be read by the prison before they are sent to my family. And the same with letters that they send to me. This can take months, and I know that there are some of my letters which have got lost completely. (Arab, Littlebourne)

Two-thirds of prisoners in all establishments, however, felt that a notable degree of racial prejudice existed amongst the inmate population. But there was a marked variation in the responses of different racial groups. White prisoners were the most likely to identify racial prejudice amongst inmates and Asians were the least likely: 82 per cent of Whites thought such prejudice existed, compared with 63 per cent of Blacks, and just four (29 per cent) of Asians. Only a minority of inmates considered this racial bias to be endemic amongst all racial groups within the inmate population.[35] For the most part racial intolerance was largely seen to be concentrated in the Black and White populations. Amongst those who felt that inmates were racially prejudiced, nine out of ten thought that Whites were prejudiced

[35] A third (35%) of all Whites thought this, a quarter (26%) of Blacks, and only one Asian.

against Blacks and three-quarters thought that Blacks were prejudiced against Whites. Yet fewer than two out of five thought that Whites or Blacks were prejudiced against Asians, and only one in five thought that Asians were prejudiced against either Whites or Blacks. Racial prejudice was thought to find expression mainly in the avoidance of contact between members of different racial groups. There was considerable agreement amongst all prisoners that racial intolerance rarely escalated to the point of physical conflict or emerged as scapegoating, although Black and White inmates reported a relatively high level of verbal aggression.

The overall majority (64 per cent) of the sample did not think that any single racial group had taken over or dominated any particular facilities in the prison. In this respect, however, greater concern was expressed at the youth custody centre than at the adult prisons. At Newfield about half of the inmates interviewed identified certain activities, services, or equipment which they thought had become monopolized by Black inmates.[36] The types of activities they were thought to dominate varied from the most conventional to the most deviant:

You find the Black guys here always choose to go on the same training courses. And I think that's because they're the best ones. (Black, Newfield)

Blacks completely dominate the pool table so that the White lads never get a look in. There is a list which you're supposed to put your name on if you want a game. But what they do is, they fix the list so that when it's your turn they say their friend was before you. (White, Newfield)

It's mainly the Black groups that do all the taxing. You tend to see the Blacks taxing Whites rather than the other way round. (Black, Newfield)

In comparison racial domination appeared to be a feature for fewer than a third of the inmates at the adult establishments. At East Bridge it was the Blacks who were again seen to be predominant, whereas at Littlebourne it was the White 'gangsters' who were said to be supreme.

The extent to which the predominance of any one racial

---

[36] A similar pattern was evident at the other youth custody centre, Duxton, where Black trainees were again depicted as the dominant group by both White and Black respondents.

group was thought to create resentment and hostility varied according to the nature of the activities and the ways in which such dominance had been achieved. In so far as it was seen to be a result of individual preferences or free choice it was not generally considered to cause any bad feeling. Discontent tended to build up when activities were monopolized by certain groups using tactics which were regarded as exploitative or intimidating, such as 'taxing', or jumping the queue for the pool table. Yet it has to be emphasized that only 16 per cent of those interviewed thought that there were any facilities which had been taken over in such a way as to cause animosity. Virtually all of these inmates, however, were concentrated at Newfield and at East Bridge, where the activities of Blacks were objected to. Hardly anyone at Littlebourne said that either they, or anyone else, resented the predominance of the Whites.

(ii) Racial Discrimination

Of crucial importance in any discussion of the inmates' perspective on race relations in prisons is their perception of the existence of racial discrimination by staff and by the prison authorities. A recurrent theme in prison officers' stereotyping of Black inmates was that they assumed racial prejudice and racial discrimination to be 'lurking around every corner'. Prisoners were asked whether they thought prison officers altered their behaviour in any way when dealing with inmates of different races. Half (53 per cent) of the White and Black inmates thought that officers did act differently in this respect, but Asians were less critical and three-quarters of them denied that this occurred. The most typical claim of inmates of all races was that prison officers were less tolerant, or more guarded and less relaxed, with ethnic minorities, especially with Black inmates. The ways in which this was said to be communicated, however, tended to be allusive, operating below the surface of day-to-day events:

It's not that they get beaten up. The screws here just don't want anything to do with them. With us they'll have a laugh and a joke, but I've never seen it with any Black con. (White, East Bridge)

It's hard to explain. It's how they talk to you rather than what they say that gives you the message. . . you can see it in their eyes. They don't like Black people. (Black, Littlebourne)

Less disquiet was felt by inmates concerning particular aspects of their interactions with staff. Overall, almost three-quarters (72 per cent) thought that prison officers helped all racial groups equally with their problems. However, Black and White prisoners were again more likely than Asian inmates to perceive patterns of discrimination. About a third of Whites and Blacks but only one Asian considered that officers did not help all racial groups equally. White inmates tended to think that Blacks received less help from prison officers than any other racial group, whereas the Blacks did not single themselves out for especially negative treatment but thought that all ethnic minorities were helped less than White prisoners. Inmates gave a variety of reasons for this less welfare-orientated approach towards ethnic minorities. They did not always assume that it was due to racial prejudice amongst staff, but occasionally acknowledged difficulties of communication and conferred some responsibility upon inmates:

It's not that the officers don't want to help them. It's just that they don't always understand what they're talking about. And the Indians don't understand them. So they go over and over the same thing until one side gives up. (White, East Bridge)

There are some officers here who don't like Blacks and wouldn't lift a finger for them. (Black, Newfield)

The staff here treat you as you treat them. Some Black guys don't want any help. They're very suspicious and give off this arrogant attitude which makes the staff keep their distance. (Black, Littlebourne)

For the most part comments about discrimination in the provision of welfare concerned the role played by prison officers. When asked about the assistance they received from the Probation and After-Care Department, the overwhelming majority (91 per cent) of inmates with sufficient experience to give a reply thought that the probation officers in their establishment treated all racial groups equally.[37] Moreover, almost everyone in the sample (94 per cent) felt that all races had an equal opportunity to benefit from education classes.

But there was less agreement regarding the question of racial discrimination in the allocation of work and the initiation of

[37] About a third of the sample felt unable to answer the question because they had experienced very little contact with the Service.

disciplinary proceedings against inmates for breaches of the prison rules. About 40 per cent of White and Black inmates claimed that, within their esablishment, ethnic minorities were racially discriminated against in the selection for particular jobs, but only four (23 per cent) Asians felt that this occurred. Similarly, in relation to prison disciplinary proceedings, none of the Asians, but a third of Black prisoners, and about a quarter of White inmates felt that the process of being placed on report, and the adjudicatory proceedings which followed, discriminated against ethnic minorities and, in particular, were biased against Blacks. It is interesting to note that a third of all prisoners who had been involved in a serious argument or fight with a member of staff or another inmate thought that they would have been treated differently had they been of a different race.

Nevertheless, it must be remembered that the majority of prisoners of all races did not claim racial discrimination in these specific areas of prison life. And in so far as unease and misgivings were expressed about some of the interactions between ethnic minorities and prison officers this was just as likely to come from the White as from the Black inmates. Moreover, very few Blacks complained that they had been discriminated against personally. Occasionally they expressed concern about their own treatment by prison staff, but were hesitant to claim that this represented racial discrimination. At the same time, however, it must be borne in mind that one of the perennial problems associated with the enforcement of all equal opportunity policies is the difficulty which individuals face in acquiring satisfactory evidence of discriminatory practices. First, it is not always possible for a prisoner to know if he is being treated differently; and second, if he does know, it is not always possible to establish that this is due to discrimination on the basis of race. We were given a number of illuminating instances:

I realised after I'd been here about a month that when this particular officer is on duty I'm always the last one out of my cell to slop out and so I'm always one of the last to get my breakfast. And it's usually cold by then . . . To tell you the truth, I don't know whether it's because I'm Black or whether the officer just doesn't like me. (Black, Newfield)

I applied for a job in the [place of work] and I was offered a job in the [another place of work]. I don't know why I was turned down because I know they were short in the [place of work], but I was so keen to get out of the Weavers that I just took what I could get . . . It crossed my mind at the time that I could have been turned down because I was Black, but there's no way of knowing. (Black, Littlebourne)

When I used to work up there I saw a lot of things. I used to hear them talking about the Blacks . . . about how they were a plague on the country and all that. When the Black guys came through they just got rid of them as quickly as they could. They'd never answer any questions for them or anything like that. I don't know if any of the Black guys ever knew they got treated differently. They probably thought they treated everybody like it. (White, East Bridge)

What is certain, however, is that Black prisoners were not, as officers were prone to claim, 'screaming racial discrimination at every opportunity'.

(iii) Alienated Minorities? The Prison System

Black inmates were frequently characterized by prison officers as presenting difficulties in prison on account of their perceived rejection of White authority. Yet the responses of Whites, Blacks, and Asians were markedly similar when they were asked whether they thought that their period in custody had 'put them off crime' and whether they thought that they had benefited in any way from their imprisonment.[38] Most typically the benefits mentioned by all groups focused upon training opportunities and the fact that removal from their usual environment enabled them to take stock and reflect upon their situation with a greater degree of clarity. Nor was there any evidence that Black prisoners were particularly hostile to prison officers. As already shown, Black prisoners perceived some difficulties in their relationships wtih staff, but they were no more likely than White inmates to claim that officers were racially prejudiced or that they acted in a discriminatory way towards them.

Contrary to the views of prison officers, White, Black, and Asian inmates were equally likely to say that they had experienced problems during their time in prison, and the sorts of difficulties they described were strikingly similar, relating

---

[38] 42% of Whites, 44% of Blacks, and half of the Asians thought that their sentence had put them off committing further crimes; and 50% of Whites, 47% of Blacks, and a third of the Asians thought that they had benefited in some way from their imprisonment.

mainly to family matters.[39] Only one in ten inmates of all races said that the main problems they had in prison involved their relationships with prison staff. In general, inmates were reticent in approaching prison staff with their problems and only a third of them said that they had discussed any of their difficulties with prison officers.[40] Despite the fact that Black inmates were slightly less likely to do this, the reasons they gave did not indicate an especial antipathy towards prison officers.[41] Like White and Asian prisoners, they tended to feel that the personal nature of their problems, and the fact that they usually concerned issues outside of the prison, meant that there was little that prison officers could do to help them. But Black inmates differed from both Whites and Asians in the extent to which they felt socially distanced from officers. None of the Asians, only one in fifteen of the Whites, but one in four of the Blacks felt that the sort of relationship they had with officers was insufficiently close or informal for them to be able to discuss their personal problems. Yet Black prisoners did not express feelings of hostility or antagonism. Indeed, more Black inmates than Whites were in favour of prison officers undertaking a welfare role.[42]

4. RACIAL GROUPING: INSULARITY AND SOLIDARITY

(i) The Nature and Functions of Racial Grouping

The cliché 'birds of a feather flock together' was often used by prison officers in their analyses of race relations in prisons.

[39] 89% of Whites, 81% of Blacks, and all of the Asians said that they had experienced problems in prison. 70% of Whites, 76% of Blacks, and two-thirds of the Asians said that the problems had been of an emotional nature, related to their homes or families.

[40] In addition, only 33% of inmates, regardless of race, had sought assistance from the Probation Service. Most typically, inmates were reluctant to involve the Probation Service because they felt that their problems were not amenable to that type of intervention.

[41] 26% of Blacks, 37% of Whites, and almost half (41%) of the Asians said that they had spoken to prison officers about their problems.

[42] 48% of Whites, 63% of Blacks, and almost all (82%) of the Asians felt that it was appropriate for prison officers to offer guidance and advice to prisoners.

Virtually all staff thought that inmates grouped together on the basis of race, although they did not suggest that such groupings were necessarily founded upon racial hostility. When they discussed racial grouping Whites were hardly ever mentioned. It was a phenomenon associated almost entirely with Black and Asian prisoners, especially the former. A factor which was identified almost exclusively with Black grouping was its potential for physical support in the event of conflict and the opportunities it provided for the exploitation of other inmates. Asian groups, on the other hand, tended more often to be portrayed as enabling a range of self-supporting services to inmates, which facilitated conformist adaptations to prison life.

This research sought to examine the extent to which these generalizations were mirrored in the perceptions held by inmates themselves about racial grouping in prisons, and their accounts of their own experiences. The responses of inmates were markedly similar to those of prison officers. Almost three-quarters of them thought that there was a tendency for inmates of the same race to form groups; most (66 per cent) thought that this did not indicate any feelings of racial hostility but represented a recognition of common bonds and shared experiences. Like prison officers, inmates at Newfield and East Bridge tended to think that Black prisoners were most likely to group together, and inmates at Littlebourne thought that Blacks and Asians were almost equally inclined to engage in such behaviour. In general, White prisoners mentioned Blacks as the most likely to form groups, much more frequently than did Blacks or Asians.[43] And again, like staff, hardly anyone referred to grouping amongst Whites.

However, the perceptions which inmates held about the nature of racial grouping were not reflected in their accounts of their own behaviour. When they were asked how and with whom they spent their time in prison, it emerged that White prisoners were far more likely than prisoners of any other race to say that they associated in racially cohesive groups. Half (51 per cent) of the White inmates said that they mixed either in defined cliques or in more loosely knit groups, compared with 31 per cent of

[43] Amongst those who identified any one race as the most likely to form groups, 75% of Whites mentioned Blacks, but only 40% of the ethnic minorities mentioned Blacks.

Blacks and three (18 per cent) Asians. Black and Asian prisoners were more likely to specify one or two particular individuals with whom they spent most of their time. Moreover, two-thirds of the Whites, but only half of the Blacks and the Asians said that they mixed exclusively with prisoners of their own race.

It is significant that half the prisoners at all three establishments who had discussed their personal problems with another inmate said that they had done so with someone of a different race from themselves. But overall Whites appeared to have been somewhat less likely than Blacks or Asians to have approached someone of a different race.[44] In another respect, too, Whites tended to be more racially insular than either Blacks or Asians. When asked whether, and with whom, they shared such items as tobacco, food, and toiletries, a third of Whites said that they did so exclusively with inmates of their own race, compared with only 13 per cent of Blacks, and three (18 per cent) Asians.

Of course, this may be explained in part by the racial composition of the prison population. This makes it statistically probable that White prisoners will come into contact more often with persons of their own race than with members of any other racial group, and that ethnic minorities will have less chance than Whites of coming into contact with persons of their own race. Nevertheless, these findings suggest that the stereotype of Blacks and Asians as having a special propensity to form racially insular groups is a distortion of reality.

It was widely believed by inmates at all establishments and of all races that group membership provided a sense of psychological security.[45] The extent to which this was translated into physical support in situations of conflict, or was used as a vehicle

[44] Of those inmates who discussed their problems with prisoners at Littlebourne: 56% did so with someone of a different race and same age (DRSA) and 17% with someone of a different race and different age (DRDA); at East Bridge 38% (DRSA), 44% (DRDA); and at Newfield 53% (DRSA). Of White inmates who discussed their problems with other prisoners, 28% (DRSA), 12% (DRDA); of Black prisoners, 53% (DRSA), 26% (DRDA); of Asian prisoners, 60% (DRSA), 40% (DRDA). These figures should be interpreted with caution because of the small numbers in each of the categories.

[45] 68% of those inmates who said that there were benefits identified this as one of them.

of exploitation, can only be understood in the context of particular prison environments.

(ii) Racial Grouping and Inmate Social Organization

In order to understand more fully the patterns of interaction which occur between different racial groups in prisons, it is necessary to look more closely at the specific contexts within which inmates of different races come into contact with one another, and the effect which the structure and organization of regimes have upon their collective adaptations to imprisonment. Social relations within prisons are obviously affected by the identities and social experiences which inmates bring with them from outside, and by the deprivations inherent in imprisonment. Carroll has suggested that the 'importation' and 'indigenous origin' models of inmate social organization should be seen as complementary, reflecting different forms of inmate organization under different structural conditions. According to Carroll, the more rigid and authoritarian the regime, the greater the feelings of deprivation and the more likely the development of inmate solidarity. Conversely, the less harsh the regime the fewer the deprivations and the greater the probability of dissonance between inmate groups, 'A worthy hypothesis, then, is that collective solidarity among prisoners is directly related to the degree of deprivation and control to which they are subject.'[46]

The three main prisons which were studied represent fundamentally different types of establishment, holding different populations for different periods of time, within a context of somewhat different regulations and routines. The purpose of this section is to consider the three prisons in some detail and to describe how the respective features of Littlebourne, Newfield, and East Bridge affect the cohesiveness and stability of racial groups and the fluidity of their boundaries. Particular attention is paid to the ways in which racial divisions can be increased or reduced by certain aspects of the organization of prison regimes and the inmate social world.

Littlebourne Littlebourne is part of the dispersal system, holding long-term prisoners in conditions of maximum security.

[46] Carroll *Hacks, Blacks and Cons*, p. 5.

During the course of the research it demonstrated a highly structured inmate social system within which it was possible to identify a hierarchy of specific inmate groups. At the top of the social order were the White professional criminals, otherwise called the 'gangsters', who had been convicted largely of manslaughter and armed robbery offences committed in the context of organized criminal activity. Many of them were known to one another outside of prison, either directly or indirectly, through their criminal networks. They saw themselves as highly skilled experts and as an experienced élite who had achieved considerable success in their careers. In consequence, they expected and demanded the respect of the 'lower classes' within the establishment—and this was usually given. They were described by staff and inmates alike as the 'top men' in the prison.

In effect a class system appeared to be in operation in which the top men acted as an entrepreneurial group dominating the illicit economy and, in consequence, determining in large measure the allocation of scarce resources. At Littlebourne there was a cash economy, paper money was not legal tender and inmates' wages were paid in coins, which could be used to purchase items from the canteen. The illicit markets also tended to be dominated by cash transactions. Participation in the illicit markets may be seen as a means of alleviating some of the deprivations associated with imprisonment. In some instances this market directly supplied goods which either were not available through legitimate channels (such as alcohol and drugs), or not normally supplied in the quantities required (such as tobacco). Alternatively for the entrepreneur the markets provided a source of coin cash, which could be used to purchase goods, such as special food or certain types of sports clothes, through legitimate prison channels. The inmate economy also enabled the provision of certain services to alleviate the tedium and monotony of the prison routine. On each wing, for example, there was a 'bookie' who accepted bets in the same way as a commercial turf accountant in the outside world. Wagers were placed in cash and winning payments were also in cash. According to a number of accounts from different sources, the stakes being played for were not small and had on occasions been measured in hundreds of pounds.

Inmates' supply of cash was primarily from three sources: prison wages, the illicit markets, and outside suppliers. Outside sources provided a large number of inmates with access to paper money. During visits £5 and £10 notes would be surreptitiously smuggled to inmates usually as gifts from their visitors. Outside suppliers served not only to inject cash into the economy but also to extract money in exchange for material goods such as drugs. Entrepreneurs also exported cash from the prison economy to outside investments and as gifts to family and friends. But as 'metal' money was the only source of legal tender within the prison, it was a constantly diminishing resource. Arrangements had to be made, therefore, to keep the economy buoyant. Hence there were the money brokers, who provided coin for paper money and vice versa at a set rate of exchange based upon the level of current demand and the difficulties of supply. At the time of the research the exchange rate was fixed at £10 paper money for £6 coin.

The gangsters did not constitute a single homogeneous group but a series of cliques or 'firms', which tended to operate their own business ventures on the different wings. Roles and relationships within and across cliques were well understood and respected, and there tended to be an atmosphere of co-operation, aided by an elaborate network of communication. Central to this was the role played by the 'runners'. These were men employed in jobs which enabled some freedom of movement outside the wing, most typically corridor cleaning, which made it possible for them to operate a courier service. They carried bets, communicated odds, transfered goods and money, and generally kept the wheels of trade turning. Prison work was circumnavigated to enable prisoners to focus attention upon their business interests. Wing cleaning was the most popular choice and was largely dominated by the gangster class because it required only a small investment of their time. But some of these prisoners did not work at all and employed other inmates who officially worked in other parts of the prison to carry out their work for them in their spare time. In keeping with a model of capitalist enterprise, the gangsters extracted the surplus value of their employees' labour, paying them only a proportion of the weekly wage, which they received in cash from the prison.

At the opposite end of the hierarchy to the gangsters were the 'nonces', men convicted of sex offences and crimes against children. Members of this group were ostracized and despised by the majority of other prisoners. But unlike their experience at other long-term prisons, sex offenders were rarely physically assaulted and generally did not have to resort to the protection of segregated confinement under Rule 43. Many of the inmates who took part in the research said that one of the costs they had to accept in exchange for the relaxed regime at Littlebourne was having to live in close quarters with men they regarded as inhuman and perverted. As the equivalent of the lumpenproletariat these men were excluded from the means of illicit production, and only occasionally were they permitted to participate as consumers. In the main they existed on the very margins of social life. Even within their own class they tended to be isolated and alone, largely because they too did not want to be closely identified with other discredited prisoners for fear of retaliation.

Between these two extremes, one cohesive and organized the other fragmented and unassimilated, were the vast majority of Littlebourne's inmates. Most of these were difficult to place within formal groups but there were two discernible collectivities of prisoners which played important roles in the power structure of the inmates' social world. The first were the 'terrorists' and the second were the Black prisoners. The former group tended to perceive themselves as political prisoners and formed separate and distinct cliques which largely opted out of operating the illicit markets. They were seen as 'hard men' who were well organized and were, therefore, not to be crossed. They used the prison economy for their own convenience but appeared to be largely self-sufficient in their adaptation to prison life. Black prisoners, however, were the equivalent of the small businessmen operating on the margins of the economy. They tended to specialize in supplying drugs and, to some extent, acting as money brokers. The gangsters generally perceived the Blacks as amateurs and tolerated their activities only within certain limits.

One of the greatest problems for staff working in maximum security dispersal prisons is gaining the compliance of long-term inmates who have little to lose. Officers at Littlebourne believed that a clearly defined hierarchy enabled them to identify those inmates who had power and influence over others in the population and with whom they could negotiate when seeking co-operation for new policies. But prison officers also identified advantages in having the gangsters, in particular, at the pinnacle of the inmate power structure. They were perceived as 'reasonable cons', prepared to play the game according to an agreed set of conventions and, in consequence, they facilitated the smooth running of the establishment. Alternative power élites were considered to be undesirable because they could not be relied upon to co-operate with staff in maintaining the current regime. Terrorist prisoners were ascribed the status of revolutionaries, dedicated to the subversion of established authority and control. Black prisoners, on the other hand, whilst not considered as committed to the destruction of all lawful governance, were regarded as internally disorganzied, ill-disciplined, and unwilling to accept any constraint upon their activities. Staff were thus prepared to co-operate in maintaining the dominance of the gangsters. They permitted them access to the prized wing cleaning jobs, which allowed them considerable 'free' time to devote to business and leisure activities, and they 'turned a blind eye' to the contracting-out of cleaning duties and to the blatant way in which the gangsters carried out their 'alternative work'. One 'bookie', for example, spent most of his day watching racing on television or studying racing papers and actually succeeded in changing his cell for one closer to the television room.

For the most part a peaceful co-existence reigned at Littlebourne between the gangster élite and the less powerful Black groups. But where certain boundaries were breached the full weight of the ruling class would descend to bring the Blacks 'into line'. Indeed this happened during the field-work. Considerable difficulty was encountered in trying to get to the precise root of the problem. But as a White gangster enigmatically put it, 'Specific individuals got out of their pram and had to be helped back in.' Allegedly, a series of warnings had been issued by the White élite which had not been heeded by the Blacks concerned. Violence was resorted to, racial divisions were heightened, and the affair escalated into virtual racial warfare. The ensuing situation was graphically described by a

Black inmate who had felt himself to be on the fringes of the events leading up to the trouble:

I don't know what it's all about but I'm getting really scared in here . . . There are about 30 Whites going around 'tooled up'. My mate told me to watch my back. He's White and he said that all of them [the Whites] were going to be lying in wait for us on the sportsfield on Sunday. So I've told my mates, my Black mates I mean . . . he took a real risk in telling me about their plans but he's a good bloke . . . No he's got to go along with the Whites, it's expected. If he doesn't, well . . . When it comes down to it like this it's strictly Whites against Blacks, even best mates against best mates, although you never actually go for your mates.

Neither side had been willing to give evidence to prison staff and since the combat had been carefully planned to avoid the presence of uniformed officers no formal action had been taken, although a Black leader was subsequently transferred from the wing.

The social organization of the inmate population at Little-bourne clearly reflected the importance of a culture imported from outside the prison walls. Yet despite the diversity of inmate groups and their differential access to power, it was possible to identify the co-existence of a different pattern of organization based upon inmate unity and solidarity. Under certain conditions, in particular, the existence of a real or imagined threat of restriction by prison staff, divisions between inmate groups would temporarily dissolve in the face of shared vulnerability. An example of this occurred when a search took place, ostensibly to discover a tool which had disappeared from one of the workshops. A notice was issued in the evening informing all prisoners that a search would be mounted the following morning starting at a particular time. That evening there was a flurry of activity to dispose of items in the cells which could result in disciplinary proceedings. The fact that St Patrick's Day was only a few days ahead ensured that stocks of prison 'hooch' were unusually high. Inmates of all races pulled together. Gallons of fermenting liquid were flushed down lavatories and supplies which were ready for consumption were hastily consumed. The next morning all inmates were locked in their cells and officers began a cell-by-cell search. It emerged, however, that the tool had been found before the raid began and, as a result, inmates started to look for the hidden agenda. According to senior staff, the search, once begun, had continued as a matter of routine in order to see what else might turn up. Nevertheless, there was a strong feeling amongst the inmates that the whole exercise had been planned to foil any St Patrick's Day celebration by Irish prisoners. Regardless of the level of sympathy extended by fellow prisoners for a St Patrick's Day party, a sense of collective victimization reigned. Staff were perceived as having played a game of cat and mouse in which the 'them and us' divide had become sharply focused.

East Bridge   The high degree of organization and continuity in the inmate social structure at Littlebourne was not mirrored in the other establishments studied. On A wing at East Bridge the illicit economy was not formally organized and there was no structure of identifiable groups within the inmate population. Being a local prison there was very little continuity in the population. The wing operated as a transit camp between the court and the training prison. Only a small and diverse group of prisoners was held back from transfer to other establishments: namely, those who needed specialist medical facilities, prisoners awaiting further court appearances, and inmates selected for particular work tasks in the prison. The high degree of unemployment for inmates on A wing resulted in many prisoners spending a vast proportion of the day in their cells. Opportunities for inmate contact during evening association were also limited since each prisoner was called for association only one evening in three. In consequence, most interaction tended to occur between prisoners sharing the same cell.

Most significantly the organization and purpose of the local prison not only made it extremely difficult for inmates to form cohesive groups but also ensured that there would be little benefit for them if they were to do so. For most inmates the knowledge that they were due for transfer encouraged them to define their time at East Bridge as transitory and to focus their attention upon the immediate practical concerns associated with their pending allocation. In addition there were definite disincentives for the men who had been picked to stay at East Bridge on the permanent work-force to engage in any kind of group behaviour which might be considered by staff as potentially troublesome. In seeking to preserve what they considered to be the privilege of staying at East Bridge, because it facilitated easy visits from their families and friends, these men tended to behave in a conformist and individualistic way.

There was a prison economy which operated to mitigate the deprivations associated with imprisonment, but there was no clearly defined or organized entrepreneurial enterprise as at Littlebourne. In the main the supply of illicit goods was a private activity and was not organized as a business. Goods were supplied largely through visits from friends and relatives, and these were consumed and traded with individuals on a personal and *ad hoc* basis. Some Black prisoners were known by other inmates to be well supplied with cannabis and to be prepared to trade. According to one Black prisoner, however, their supply was intended primarily for their own use, to 'normalize' their existence, and to help them get through their sentence. They would exchange any surplus they had either for cash to use in the canteen or for tobacco. Obviously certain individuals had greater access to valued goods than others, but the social organization of the market was in a constant process of change in accordance with the ebb and flow of the population.

Newfield   The social organization of the inmate culture at Newfield youth custody centre incorporated elements found at Littlebourne and at East Bridge. Three distinctive features of this establishment shaped the pattern of inmate relations: first, the age of the inmate population; second, the relatively short length of the sentences being served (rarely over eighteen months); and third, the fact that most inmates were drawn from the London area.

All inmates were under the age of 21 and their interactions with one another reflected their lack of sophistication and maturity. Modest supplies of illicit goods made their way into Newfield, largely for individual consumption, and there was very little organized trading. It was more a case of goods and services being extracted from people by the stronger exploiting the weak. This was done either by means of a 'protection system', where individuals paid to avoid violence, or by direct theft. An inmate's physical size and his reputation as a 'hard man' were consequently crucial features in determining his position in the power structure. Those who aspired to power tended to gather around a tough leader, but there was no clearly defined group structure or permanency of membership. No single gang controlled the whole establishment, rather there were a number of competing and shifting factions. Those who extorted money or tobacco from the less robust inmates were not necessarily those who bullied others to relinquish their place on the rota to play billiards. Relations between groups could be either competitive, resulting in threatening negotiations and even physical violence, or co-operative, with different groups accepting different territorial claims.

From reports by Black and White inmates and from prison staff, Black prisoners frequently assumed positions of dominance within the inmate social structure. Resentment was expressed about Black inmates monopolizing the best seats in the television room and constantly talking to one another in loud voices throughout programmes. The Black trainees, in turn, readily admitted that they tended to dominate the pool table to the extent that some White inmates were reticent to play. But it was not the case that only Black groups engaged in exploitative behaviour. In the first period of field-work at Newfield both Black and to a lesser extent White groups were actively engaged in bullying and extortion. But those who exploited others did not discriminate on the grounds of race: Black groups exploited both Black and White prisoners, as did the White groups. Nor was the power enjoyed by the dominant groups all embracing. Their spheres of influence did not extend to controlling access to what were considered to be the best jobs in the prison and they did not necessarily dominate the supply of illicit goods.

In general most youth custody trainees at Newfield tried to cope with bullying by seeking to avoid contact with the powerful set. When, for example, a particular group was dominating the pool table, other inmates tended to avoid playing. Similarly if a group insisted on claiming particular seats in the television room, others would either not watch television or, if the programme were sufficiently important, sit elsewhere.

There were, however, periods in which no groups held dominant sway at Newfield. Twelve months later, during the second period of observation, there was no discernible group engaged in bullying or extortion. According to inmates' accounts, a Black group had been engaged in these activities but had so overstepped the mark that a number of strong White inmates had gathered together to put an end to this exploitation. But the White group did not take over where the Black group had left off. In this instance they felt that their motivation in challenging the Black group was not based upon any desire to supersede them but was borne out of frustration. As one of the White protesters explained:

It had got ridiculous. You couldn't leave your peter for two minutes without one of them nipping in and nicking the batteries out of your radio ... I'm not interested in being a Baron or whatever they call them. This is my first time inside and it's going to be my last. I don't want any trouble, just do my time and get out. But there's only so much you can take and it had just got right out of order.

Two explanations suggest why membership of these 'power groups' should be so fluid: first, there is the inevitable and regular turnover of the population; and second, many inmates were known to one another outside the prison and this tended to obscure the boundaries between the prison-based groups. Staff at Newfield recognized that the ways in which inmate power was achieved, the form in which it was expressed, and its fluctuating and factional manifestation represented a fundamental challenge to their authority and undermined the maintenance of good order and discipline. Hence they actively discouraged such activities and would, on occasion, take action to discipline or remove inmates who enaged in them.

5
Racial Discrimination in Prisons

Racial prejudice and discrimination are widely acknowledged to exist in British society. Individual instances are known to occur within all large organizations and the Prison Service would not claim to be an exception. The purpose of this chapter is to examine whether such behaviour is endemic within prisons. The question of racial discrimination is considered in four areas of prison life: in disciplinary proceedings; in the written assessments held on inmate records about their anticipated behaviour and training needs in prison; in the processes of wing and cell allocation; and in the allocation of labour. But first the question of definition and proof must be addressed.

1. PROBLEMS OF IDENTIFICATION AND PROOF

Both the prevalence of racial stereotyping and the existence of racial prejudice amongst prison staff have already been described in Chapter 3. But what about racial discrimination in prisons? It may be argued that attitudes are one thing and behaviour another. Some Prison Department officials, governors, and other prison staff considered that it was acceptable, even if undesirable, for prison staff to have racist attitudes, as long as they acted in a professional way in their dealings at work, 'After all, every man is entitled to his own opinion.' Although the Prison Department in its generic training programme seeks to confront racist attitudes, the policy statement does not explicitly demand that prison officers who hold such views change their opinions about or attitudes towards ethnic minority prisoners. Its appeal is directed towards the elimination of discriminatory behaviour.

The question of whether racial discrimination exists in prisons raises the fundamental issue of how to identify and prove that it is happening. How a researcher or any other investigator identifies that discrimination is taking place is not at all straightforward. In the first place victims of discrimination are not always aware that they are being discriminated against. This is particularly common in the case of indirect discrimination. The researcher may find himself or herself in the invidious position of attributing racial discrimination to behaviour which is seen by neither the discriminators nor the victims, as discriminatory in intent or effect. A further problem, which is especially common in the identification of direct discrimination, is that of causal attribution. An example of this was encountered at Newfield, where one Black trainee was consistently being left locked in his cell by his labour party officer while other inmates on the party were being unlocked to go to work. Although the trainee felt convinced that the grounds on which he was being kept off the party were racial, he did not feel able to make any complaint because he believed that he could not prove it. In his view, any formal complaint would have been met by the labour party officer claiming either that he had 'forgotten' that this trainee was on his party or that he 'did not need a full complement of the party' during that period. In this way much racial discrimination may remain hidden. But even if the victim can prove that he has been discriminated against on racial grounds, he may feel that it is not in his interests to make a complaint:

When it comes down to it you don't have a leg to stand on. They've got you, however you look at it—they can call you Nigger and kick your arse around. If you complain they only define you as a troublemaker. They see you as just screaming racial prejudice and it fulfils all their stereotypes of you and keeps them happy. Basically, you can't win. The best thing is to just sit quietly and take it. (Black, Littlebourne)

For these reasons, it is particularly hard to prove that direct discriminatory actions have been motivated by racial consider- ations. Inevitably evidence of a person's intentions is largely anecdotal and, as such, is often regarded as unreliable. Thus, it is difficult enough to cite individual instances let alone to demonstrate their systemic application.

2. RACIAL DISCRIMINATION IN DISCIPLINARY
PROCEEDINGS

It was not possible to undertake a full-scale study to assess the influence of all the factors which affect disciplinary proceedings in prisons. In consequence what may be said about race relations in this context must be somewhat fragmentary and preliminary.

Disciplinary proceedings may be taken against an inmate by an officer for any infraction of the Prison Rules. These include using violence against other inmates or against staff; using insolent or abusive language to an officer; refusing orders; creating a disturbance; damaging prison property; or being in possession of contraband items, such as money, drugs, weapons, or other inmates' property. Once disciplinary proceedings have been initiated, each individual case is referred for adjudication before the governor and he or she may refer it to the Board of Visitors if the charge is considered to be of a sufficiently serious nature. If the prisoner is found guilty the adjudicating body is empowered, within certain limits laid down in the Prison Rules, to award an appropriate punishment. Usually this will take the form of loss of association, loss of earnings, or loss of remission. With such wide discretion, both to charge and punish, it is possible that racial discrimination could operate at various stages of the proceedings.

Carroll, in his study of race relations in an American maximum security prison, concluded that significant differences existed in the disciplinary proceedings initiated against Black and White inmates.[1] With regard to formal disciplinary action he discovered that Black prisoners were reported more frequently for disciplinary infractions. He did not, however, find any evidence to suggest that they were being punished more severely than White prisoners by the Disciplinary Board. Carroll postulated that the disproportionate number of Black inmates against whom disciplinary action was taken was to some extent due to the perceptions of the custodians, who saw Black prisoners as dangerous and conspiring revolutionaries. These shared conceptions, in his view, disposed the custodians to a

[1] Carroll, *Hacks, Blacks and Cons*, pp. 115–45.

pattern of closer surveillance and control of Black inmates than of White inmates. In consequence, he argued, many orders issued by prison guards were likely to be seen as arbitrary and capricious by Black prisoners, thus provoking a hostile response. The hypothesis was that of a self-fulfilling prophecy.

There have been no studies of this kind in prisons in England and Wales. The Psychology Unit at East Bridge had initiated a study but it had been 'put on ice' due to the complexity of the variables involved. Nevertheless some monitoring of disciplinary offences (but not of adjudicatory awards) in relation to race had been carried out at Littlebourne, Newfield, and Duxton. What emerged was a rather confusing and contradictory picture. At both Newfield and Littlebourne the rate of disciplinary action taken against ethnic minority inmates was not out of proportion to their numbers in the establishment. At Duxton, on the other hand, the race relations laision officer concluded that 'ethnic minority discipline reports continue to remain high in comparison to the establishment's ethnic population'. Here ethnic minority inmates accounted for 52 per cent of the disciplinary reports filed in 1985 yet only constituted between 35 and 39 per cent of the total population.

The results of this monitoring should, however, be interpreted with great caution since a number of fundamental questions remain unanswered. As the race relations liaison officer at Duxton recognized, the data do not, for example, take account of persistent offending. Nor do they indicate how many of the reports were filed against how many or how few inmates. And there was little information regarding the nature or severity of the infractions. But, perhaps most importantly, any monitoring which is based simply upon counting the number of disciplinary reports filed against inmates and which fails to pay heed to the real level of offending behaviour by inmates of different races, is liable to be misleading. The number of disciplinary reports in any establishment cannot represent an accurate reflection of the number of infractions committed by inmates, since much of this behaviour goes unobserved and many other incidents are responded to informally by staff. The absence of such information makes it impossible to assess whether differences in the rates of disciplinary reports recorded against inmates of different racial origins reflect actual variations in inmates' behaviour, variations in the recording practices of prison staff, or, indeed, a combination of these factors.

Having said this, however, field-work carried out at the three main establishments did indicate that there were some differences in the responses of staff to infractions committed by inmates of different racial origins, although the number of cases studied was too small for any firm conclusions to be drawn. The method used was that of a self-report study. Each inmate who was interviewed was asked whether he had ever been involved in a serious argument or fight with prison staff or with other inmates. If so, he was asked whether staff had intervened and what action, if any, had been taken against him as a result.

Only 30 inmates (20 per cent of the interview sample) claimed that they had been involved in serious confrontations with staff and 56 inmates (40 per cent) said that they had experienced violent conflict with other inmates. There were no differences in the proportions of White and Black inmates involved in such incidents, although Asian prisoners were under-represented. Moreover the descriptions of incidents given by the inmates involved suggested that there were no qualitative differences in the nature of the violent confrontations experienced by inmates of different racial origins. Yet differences did emerge in the subsequent action taken by prison staff. Although officers intervened in only 38 per cent of all the incidents between inmates which the respondents mentioned, they did so more often when one or more of the combatants was Black or Asian. Indeed it was claimed that staff had intervened in half of all the fights and arguments in which ethnic minority inmates said they had been involved, but in only about a quarter of those reported by White inmates. Formal action followed in virtually all of the incidents in which staff intervened. Thus, a greater proportion of ethnic minority than White inmates were referred for adjudication: 15 out of the 30 (50 per cent) incidents reported by ethnic minority inmates, as opposed to 5 out of the 26 (19 per cent) reported by Whites. A similar picture was evident when confrontations with staff were examined. Formal action was said to have been taken twice as frequently against ethnic minority inmates as against White inmates.[2] These preliminary findings

---

[2] Five of the 14 White inmates (36%), compared with 11 of the 16 ethnic minority inmates (69%) had formal action taken against them.

indicate that further research into this very complex area of interaction is called for.

3. RACIAL DISCRIMINATION IN WRITTEN ASSESSMENTS (STANDARD CLASSIFICATION FORMS)

The use of racially discriminatory language and the stereotyping of ethnic minority inmates in written documents is firmly prohibited in the Prison Department's policy statement. All race relations liaison officers and many senior staff had made considerable efforts to discourage racially demeaning and stereotypical depictions in Prison Department records. An examination of the Standard Classification Forms which had been completed for 1,255 medium-term and long-term prisoners revealed that, whilst they have been largely successful in eliminating the use of derogatory language, it has proved more difficult to excise negative racial stereotypes from assessments.[3] Although there were some instances in which the race of the prisoner was referred to, such references were, for the most part, not derogatory, 'He is a 34-year old Jamaican, cohabiting with a woman . . .', or, 'This 47-year old Pakistani is a diabetic . . .'. Occasionally, however, comments were overtly demeaning. At one establishment a Black inmate was referred to as, 'a West Indian waster'; another was described as having given, 'the impression in the interview of a quiet respectful young man, not of the usual West Indian type'; and one report said of an Asian inmate, 'He has little to offer this country, but sadly cannot be deported because he has a British passport.' The officer who completes the Standard Classification Form is required to assess the inmate in terms of his propensity, to 'seek staff approval', to be 'self-reliant', 'independent of other inmates', 'amenable to authority', 'controlled', 'acceptable', to 'remain in touch', and 'be stable'. The inmate's training needs are assessed on the basis of the officer's perceptions of his educational level, his work patterns, his working skills, and personal insight.

Although the majority of all racial groups received positive

[3] For an explanation of how this work was carried out see ch. 1.

assessments with regard to their anticipated behaviour in prison, racial stereotypes were nevertheless reflected in the way inmates of different racial origins were ranked. On every dimension more Asians received higher ratings than Whites, and more Whites received higher ratings than Blacks. Black inmates were significantly more likely than any other racial group to be assessed as 'unlikely to care about staff opinion'; to be 'resistant' rather than 'amenable' to authority; to be 'aggressive' rather than 'controlled'; and to 'arouse hostility' rather than 'be acceptable'.[4] At the opposite end of the spectrum, Asians were generally regarded as apt to conform, likely to obey regulations, and unlikely to cause trouble. A similar pattern emerged with regard to officers' assessments of inmates' training needs. A higher proportion of Asians than Whites or Blacks was rated as possessing both satisfactory work patterns and working skills.[5] Black inmates, on the other hand, were most often assessed as needing to develop their work patterns and improve their skills.[6]

It may be argued that the written assessments made by prison officers do not represent an undue propensity to resort to stereotypic depictions but constitute justified predictions made on the basis of the inmate's record. It was true that the assessments made by officers, both about the likely behaviour of inmates and their training needs, reflected information at their disposal.

Thus, inmates whose records showed that they had not received or had not completed vocational training outside tended more often to be rated as needing to improve their working skills than those who had completed their vocational

[4] In the following statistics $df = 1$ and $p < 0.001$ unless otherwise stated. *Those unlikely to care/seek approval from staff*: Black/White $\chi^2 = 15.69$; Black/Asian $\chi^2 = 32.14$; White/Asian $\chi^2 = 14.29$. *Those likely to be resistant/amenable to authority*: Black/White $\chi^2 = 16.78$; Black/Asian $\chi^2 = 19.43$; White/Asian $\chi^2 = 5.77$ $p < 0.02$. *Those likely to be aggressive/controlled*: Black/White $\chi^2 = 11.42$; Black/Asian $\chi^2 = 14.14$; White/Asian $\chi^2 = 4.49$ $p < 0.02$. *Those likely to be hostile/acceptable*: Black/White $\chi^2 = 4.44$ $p < 0.05$; Black/Asian $\chi^2 = 10.89$; White/Asian $\chi^2 = 5.23$ $p < 0.05$.

[5] *Needing to develop work patterns*: Asians 30%; Whites 46%; Blacks 57%, $\chi^2 = 20.15$ $df = 2$ $p < 0.001$. *Needing to improve work skills*: Asians 47%; Whites 57%; Blacks 70%. $\chi^2 = 17.48$ $df = 2$ $p < 0.001$.

[6] *Needing to develop work patterns*: Black/White $\chi^2 = 7.88$ $df = 1$ $p < 0.01$; Black/Asian $\chi^2 = 18.69$ $df = 1$ $p < 0.001$. *Needing to improve work skills*: Black/White $\chi^2 = 10.87$ $df = 1$ $p < 0.001$; Black/Asian $\chi^2 = 14.79$ $df = 1$ $p < 0.001$.

training.[7] Similarly, a much higher proportion of inmates who had disciplinary offences recorded against them during previous periods in custody, or who had current or previous convictions for violence, were assessed as less amenable to authority, less likely to seek staff approval, and more likely to be aggressive than those who had not. Yet clear racial differences were still apparent even when these background factors were taken into account. For example, when only those inmates who had completed their vocational training were considered, three-quarters of the Asian inmates, two-thirds of the White inmates, but only half of the Blacks were assessed as possessing sufficient working skills. Similarly, amongst those inmates who were recorded as having held a job for over three years, only a quarter of the Asians, a third of the Whites, but as many as half of the Blacks were assessed as being in need of help to develop their work patterns.

There were similar racial differences when comparisons were made between officers' assessments of prisoners' anticipated behaviour in prison and inmates' records. For example, of those prisoners who had disciplinary offences recorded against them during previous spells in custody, none of the Asians, but 27 per cent of the Whites, and as many as 44 per cent of the Blacks were assessed as being resistant to authority.[8]

It must, however, be borne in mind that a larger proportion of Blacks than White or Asian inmates were under the age of 30, and that age rather than race may account for officers' assessments of Black inmates as being more prone to present with behavioural problems. In general, inmates under the age of 30 were more likely than those aged over 30 to receive negative assessments. Nevertheless, a preliminary analysis, controlling for age, revealed that even within these age-bands significant differences remained between inmates of different races on a

----

[7] Need for improved working skills: 66% of those who had not received or completed vocational training. 36% of those who had completed vocational training. $\chi^2 = 67.66$ $df = 1$ $p < 0.001$.

[8] When an analysis was made by race of those who had current or previous convictions for violence, the differences still remained statistically significant. *Unlikely to care/seek approval*: $\chi^2 = 15.97$ $df = 2$ $p < 0.001$. *Resistant/amenable to authority*: $\chi^2 = 13.43$ $df = 2$ $p < 0.001$. *Agressive/controlled*: $\chi^2 = 8.35$ $df = 2$ $p < 0.02$.

number of ratings, including: levels of resistance to authority; seeking approval from staff; and liability to be controlled or aggressive.[9]

4. RACIAL DISCRIMINATION IN THE ALLOCATION OF LIVING ACCOMMODATION

Among the controversial issues raised in virtually all debates on race relations is the question of numbers: whether there should be any restrictions placed on the numbers of ethnic minorities permitted in any social context, or any attempt to concentrate or disperse them within the majority population. These concerns were present in the minds of most prison staff, particularly in relation to Black inmates. As has already been mentioned, more than half of the prison officers thought that the proportion of Black inmates should be strictly limited within individual establishments, yet only 20 per cent of them wanted such restrictions to apply to Asian prisoners. The main argument was that when the Black population reached a certain level power struggles inevitably broke out with the White prisoners.

Prison officers have little control over the numbers of ethnic minority inmates allocated to their establishment. Where they do have considerable control, however, is in exercising their discretion to distribute the ethnic minority population between wings, and in allocating them to particular landings and cells. It was also stated at one of the prisons that the reason why they rarely had any trouble with Black inmates was because it was stemmed before it had a chance to take root. This, they said, was achieved by the transfer officer shipping some of them out to other establishments as soon as their numbers were thought to have become too high. However, there was no way of gauging how often this took place.

Interviews were conducted with nine prison officers responsible for cell allocation at the five prisons, and informal discussions were held with other officers who were responsible for allocating prisoners to wings. Four of the nine officers claimed that when cells became vacant prisoners were allocated

[9] *Unlikely to care/seek approval:* $\chi^2 = 9.15$ $df = 1$ $p < 0.01$. *Resistant/amenable:* $\chi^2 = 6.85$ $df = 1$ $p < 0.01$. *Agressive/controlled:* $\chi^2 = 3.98$ $df = 1$ $p < 0.05$.

to them purely at random and that no other factors, including the inmates' racial origin, intruded upon the decision. The other five officers said that they took into account a number of criteria in reaching their decisions. Amongst the factors which they considered were the age, offence, character, and racial origin of the inmate. For example, one officer said that he tried to locate older inmates together; and another that he exercised caution in the placement of sex offenders. At more than one establishment there was an attempt to place weaker inmates near the staff office and to keep strong or 'stroppy' ones away from powerful groups. At all of the establishments at least one officer responsible for cell allocation claimed that he dispersed ethnic minorities and, in particular, Black inmates. The reasons they gave for this, however, varied at the different establishments. One allocating officer rationalized the dispersal of Black inmates on the grounds that they were 'noisy and tend to attract groups which create tensions and can only lead to trouble'. Another felt that Black inmates 'try to take over the wash-up facilities', that 'they are slow and take their time' and that 'the White inmates get fed up of it'. The allocating officer at another prison stated:

You have to try to disperse them on the wing. We've had them together before and have had nothing but trouble . . . one area on፡፡ became a virtual 'no go' area for everyone, there were drugs and everything. Blacks are the main source of drugs in prison . . . they have different customs too, the smell of their curries [on the wing] drives off the Whites and all but the bravest staff.

It also emerged that racial dislike or racial prejudice on the part of inmates was, for some of these allocating officers, a sufficient reason for allowing cell changes. Five of them had been faced with objections from White inmates about their proximity to Blacks or Asians and all had acquiesced to a change of cell on the grounds of good management.

There was also some evidence to suggest that the policy of transferring prisoners between wings or to another prison in order to maintain good order and discipline could result in a degree of racial discrimination. Informal discussions with staff revealed that in situations of potential or actual conflict administrative convenience dictated that those who were least powerful or least numerous suffered the disadvantage of the transfer. It was often pointed out that the staff had no other option. Several cases came to light where ethnic minority inmates had been transferred despite the fact that it was generally acknowledged by both staff and inmates that it was the White prisoners who had initiated the conflict. In one instance a situation developed after a White prisoner had assaulted a Black. This resulted in a build-up of racial tension between a large and powerful group of Whites and a much smaller group of Blacks. The staff sought to defuse it by transferring one of the Black leaders because the only alternative was the far more intractable problem of dealing with the dominant White group. This dilemma is perhaps reflected in the findings of a study by a prison psychologist in the same institution. He analysed the records of adjudications of incidents which involved fights between inmates of different races and concluded that:

Although they did not reveal any racial content in the account of events, there is reason to believe, from an inmate source, that one fight involved personal dislike partly based on cultural differences. This resulted in the minority inmate being removed to another wing, and there was another near incident on the same wing which was prevented by a minority inmate being transferred to a different wing.

It should be emphasized that the criteria informing these decisions inevitably disadvantage those inmates who wield the least power. This in these instances Blacks were not necessarily being moved on account of racial prejudice *per se*, but on account of their status as members of a relatively powerless minority group. On this premise it could be argued that if Black inmates were to form the dominant group White prisoners would be moved to maintain good order. In other words, in situations of conflict, these dynamics may work to the disadvantage of any racial group, including Whites.

5. RACIAL DISCRIMINATION IN THE ALLOCATION OF INMATES TO JOBS AND TRAINING COURSES

The 1983 policy statement enjoins governors to ensure that 'all jobs, tasks, training courses, and activities generally are at all times—so far as it is practicable and sensible—distributed broadly in proportion to the ethnic mix of the population'.

Each establishment within the prison system is bound by a set of rules and procedures designed to ensure, as far as possible, efficiency and fairness in the labour allocation process. There are several formal criteria, such as those relating to security risk and medical fitness, which limit the allocation of inmates to specific jobs, but these are not seen to impinge greatly upon the otherwise disrectionary process of decision-making.

At each prison a Labour Board is appointed with responsibility for the 'hiring' and 'firing' of inmates. There are variations in the composition and procedures of the Labour Boards at different establishments, but their basic tasks remain the same. Boards regularly receive notice of all the vacancies on the various work parties in the prison and it is their duty to allocate each sentenced inmate shortly after his reception into prison to an appropriate job; it is also their responsibility to deal with requests from inmates for changes of work party; and with requests from supervisors to remove or sack 'unsatisfactory' inmates.

This research explored the extent to which the policy directive and the Labour Boards have succeeded in ensuring that there is no racial discrimination, either direct or indirect, in the procedures or outcomes of the labour allocation system. Evidence was gathered from five different sources: from a study carried out by the Psychology Unit at East Bridge; monitoring undertaken at Newfield and Duxton by the race relations liaison officers; an analysis of the labour allocation history of the current inmate population at Littlebourne; interviews with work supervisors; and observations of the work of the various Labour Boards.

In order to demonstrate whether or not there is racial discrimination in the process of allocating prison labour, it is necessary to discover whether there is a measure of consensus amongst staff and inmates about which are the 'best' and which are the 'worst' jobs. If, for example, there was no such consensus amongst inmates of different races, any differences in the proportions being assigned to different work tasks could be the result of personal preferences rather than discriminatory behaviour.

Inmates' assessments of which were the best and which were the worst jobs were usually made on the basis of the 'perks' attached to particular tasks. Thus, opinion varied, to some extent, between the three prisons. In general there was far more agreement about which were the worst jobs than about which were the best. The industrial workshops were by far the most unpopular jobs. This, it was claimed, was due to the high degree of staff supervision and the inevitable restrictions placed upon prisoners' mobility in this type of work.

The most frequently mentioned best jobs were orderly tasks and kitchen work. The popularity of these tasks emanated from the access which these jobs afforded to the 'little luxuries' of prison life. It was widely known that some prisoners in orderly positions enjoyed the privilege of sitting down for a cup of coffee and a cigarette with their supervising officer, and that those who worked in the reception area of the prison were, from time to time, allowed to smoke on the job the excess tobacco or cigarettes confiscated from new receptions. Other orderly tasks were said to provide ready access to classified information regarding, for example, parole recommendations or impending tranfers of prisoners. Kitchen work was rated highly by prisoners for two reasons. First, the long hours worked in the kitchen provided a welcome break from the monotony of life on the wing. Second, there was the added attraction of being able to smuggle out items of food and, in particular, the essential ingredients of tinned fruit, sugar, and yeast for the brewing of prison 'hooch'.

At Littlebourne wing cleaning, laundry work, and outdoor tasks were also seen as prize jobs. The popularity of wing cleaning and outdoor tasks was directly related to the opportunities afforded inmates who held these positions to conduct business on the illicit market. Laundry work, on the other hand, enabled inmates to wash and care for their own clothes and launder on contract for other inmates either to pay off debts which had been accrued or in exchange for services to be rendered. In all three establishments there were no consistent differences of opinion between racial groups in their assessments of best and worst jobs.

On the whole inmates tended not to be aware of any racial discrimination in the labour allocation process. Occasionally comments were made about the absence of ethnic minority inmates on the hotplate, in the laundry, or in the kitchen, or about their over-representation in certain workshops, such as the weavers' shop or metalwork shop at Littlebourne. But inmates admitted that many of these observations were based on hearsay or rumour and very few of them directly attributed these disproportions to racial discrimination. In all, only a third of the inmates felt that racial discrimination operated in the allocation of labour at their own prison. Nevertheless the first indication of potential discrimination came when inmates were asked whether or not they had exercised any choice over their own job assignment. As many as 71 per cent of White inmates reported that they had exercised some choice over their current job, compared with only 56 per cent of Black inmates, and 31 per cent of Asian inmates.[10]

Some useful data on the allocation of labour had been collected by the Psychology Unit at East Bridge. Over a period of four and a half months between March and August 1985 they monitored the proportions of ethnic minority inmates assigned by the Labour Boards to three main categories of work party: the workshops; off-wing work parties, such as the works, yards, and kitchen; and jobs on the wing, such as cleaning and hotplate tasks. This study demonstrated that there was a significantly higher proportion of inmates of 'West Indian' origin being allocated to workshops or left unemployed, and a significantly lower proportion being allocated to off-wing parties or on-wing jobs.[11] It also emerged that inmates from other ethnic minority groups were significantly more likely to be allocated to workshops, although significantly less likely to be unemployed. There were a number of off-wing parties and many off-wing orderly jobs, such as the bath house, the officers' club, the reception, and red-band (trustee) jobs, to which either very small numbers of inmates from the ethnic minorities had been allocated or, indeed, none at all.

The Psychology Unit also monitored the ethnic origin of inmates who were working in four workshops and on three work

[10] The figure for Asian inmates should be treated with some caution since half of the Asian sample came from East Bridge, where least choice was reported by all inmates.
[11] Internal report: $\chi^2 = 20.84$ $df = 6$ $p < 0.01$.

parties, representing a cross-section of the work opportunities available in the prison. Monitoring was carried out once a week for four consecutive weeks and then once a month for three months. This provided seven 'snapshots' of the racial composition of each of these seven work groups. They revealed that over this period of time the racial composition of each of these shops and parties remained relatively consistent, even where there was a high turnover of prisoners. Two of the seven workplaces stood out as having a very small representation of ethnic minority inmates: the laundry and the bookbinders. Although various tentative explanations, unrelated to the issue of racial discrimination, were put forward for this bias, the findings were regarded as being of sufficient concern to require further action on the part of the Race Relations Committee. They decided: first, to monitor labour allocation on a regular basis; second, to seek an explanation for the racial imbalance in workshops and work parties; and finally, to try to redress the balance of ethnic minority inmates in at least one of the parties on which they were consistently under-represented, with a view to taking formal action if there was any resistance from the supervisor.

Further evidence of racial imbalance in the labour allocation process emerged from a study of the job assignment back-records of 386 inmates held at Littlebourne on the 10 April 1986.[12] Information was gathered for each inmate about the number of his job changes; where he had previously worked in the prison; the time and proportion of his sentence spent in these previous jobs; and the nature of his current job. Thus, a comparison was made of the prison employment records of inmates of different racial origins over the whole period of their time spent at Littlebourne. One obvious factor which may influence job assignments in prison is the length of time inmates have spent within the establishment: the longer an inmate has been there the greater his opportunity to achieve one of the more prized work tasks. This factor was controlled by comparing the records of inmates who had spent similar amounts of time at Littlebourne. Although no racial differences

[12] The records of a further 17 inmates held at Littlebourne on this date were not analysed either because their records were incomplete or because they had spent the whole of their time at Littlebourne in the segregation unit.

emerged with regard to the number of job changes which inmates had experienced, a clear racial imbalance was discovered in the nature of both their current and previous jobs—an imbalance which remained constant regardless of the length of time they had spent in the establishment.

For the purpose of analysis it was decided to use inmates' own ratings of the prestige of work tasks. Again these were divided into two groups: the 'best' and 'worst' jobs. All the industrial workshop tasks were rated amongst the worst jobs; the best jobs included orderly posts, kitchen work, wing cleaning, laundry, and outdoor jobs. There were no statistically significant differences in the proportion of White (42 per cent) and ethnic minority (53 per cent) inmates who were employed in the workshops. But ethnic minority inmates were significantly less likely than Whites to be currently employed in what were considered to be the best jobs. Indeed, only 7 ethnic minority inmates (14 per cent) were engaged on work parties which fell within the best job category, compared with 149 White inmates (45 per cent).[13] Moreover, the 7 ethnic minority inmates who were employed in best jobs were not evenly dispersed across these favoured tasks: 6 of them being engaged on wing cleaning and 1 in the laundry. In other words, there were no ethnic minority inmates in any of the orderly jobs, outdoor work parties, or in the kitchen.

It was striking that an examination of the previous prison jobs held by inmates over their period of stay at Littlebourne demonstrated the same pattern of work assignment. None of the ethnic minority inmates had ever been employed in orderly or outdoor work tasks. Only one Black inmate was recorded as having been employed in the kitchen and he had remained in this post for only three months. Nor was there any evidence to suggest that this situation has changed over time. Indeed, a snapshot picture taken of the racial composition of the work parties at Littlebourne in March 1985 showed that no ethnic minority inmates were employed in orderly or kitchen tasks and only one was engaged on an outdoor work party.

Although ethnic minorities were under-represented in these highly favoured jobs they were significantly over-represented on

---

[13] Comparing best job with all other work tasks. $\chi^2 = 14.3$ $df = 1$ $p < 0.001$.

the vocational training courses.[14] It may be argued that this is because inmates of different racial origins are exercising different preferences between taking good jobs and enrolling on training courses. But this would imply that they are able to exercise a degree of free choice. Discussion on the matter with staff and inmates indicated that this was not the case. The best jobs were largely closed to ethnic minorities, both through pressures for exclusion from dominant White inmates and through the preferences of supervisors. If ethnic minorities sought to escape from the worst jobs, their realistic options were limited to vocational training and occasionally to full-time education.

Limitations of time and resources meant that comparable studies of labour allocation at Duxton, Wilding, and Newfield could not be undertaken. At two of these establishments, however, incidents were noted in which the race relations liaison officers had found it necessary to urge supervisors to enrol more ethnic minorities and, in one case, to bar the allocation of any more Black trainees to a general labour party which was described as a 'mop-up' job. At both establishments efforts had been made to monitor the racial composition of workshops and work parties. But the data had not been systematically recorded and therefore no firm conclusions could be drawn.

The most convincing evidence of racial bias in the labour allocation process was generated from the interviews conducted with 50 work supervisors from all five establishments, representing a cross-section of the work opportunities in each prison.[15] For ease of analysis, the 50 work supervisors were divided into three broad categories: those in charge of 'popular' jobs; those in charge of 'unpopular' jobs; and instructors responsible for vocational training courses. The categorization of a job as popular or unpopular varied to some extent between individual prisoners, staff, and establishments. The analysis was, therefore, based upon what was deemed to be the broad

[14] 33% of ethnic minorities were in full-time education and vocational training compared with 13% of Whites. $\chi^2 = 6.05$ $df = 1$ $p < 0.02$.

[15] Those interviewed included 14 workshop supervisors, 2 supervisors of outdoor work parties, 6 wing cleaning officers, 2 laundry supervisors, 5 works supervisors, 5 kitchen supervisors, 2 mess supervisors, 6 orderly supervisors, and 8 vocational training instructors.

consensus. As a result, workshops, outdoor work parties, and wing cleaning, were classified as unpopular jobs; and orderly posts, kitchen, mess, works, and laundry parties were categorized as popular jobs.[16]

A calculation was made of the proportion of ethnic minority inmates employed on each job in relation to their numbers in the establishment. Each supervisor was then asked whether this was the usual proportion on his party and how many ethnic minority inmates were currently employed in positions of responsibility. Of the 20 supervisors of popular jobs, only 20 per cent had a proportionate representation of ethnic minorities in their parties. The remaining 80 per cent had either a below-average representation or no ethnic minority inmates at all. In striking contrast, none of the 22 supervisors of unpopular jobs reported having no ethnic minority inmates in their work-force, and a third had an over-representation. Among the 8 vocational training instructors there was considerable variation: 3 had no ethnic minorities on their courses, but 2 had an over-representation. When asked whether the current proportion of ethnic minority inmates on their parties represented the usual pattern for their work-forces, 82 per cent said that it did.

It is interesting to note the types of jobs in which ethnic minorities were greatly under-represented. Not one of the orderly officers had an ethnic minority inmate on his work-force and 5 out of the 6 stated that this was the usual pattern. Furthermore, two of the five catering officers had no one from the ethnic minorities, the remaining 3 having a below-average representation. All these supervisors claimed that this was typical. In addition, 2 catering officers, 1 works officer, 1 laundry officer, and 2 vocational training instructors stated that they usually had no ethnic minority inmates on their parties. Thus, a total of 11 officers or instructors did not usually have any ethnic minority inmates on their parties and these included 9 (45 per cent) of the 20 supervisors of the popular jobs.

The message, it would appear, is quite clear. Racial

[16] Unlike other establishments wing cleaning and outdoor work were regarded as popular jobs at Littlebourne. This did not skew the main findings of this part of the study since no outdoor works supervisors were interviewed at Littlebourne and we interviewed only 2 cleaning officers, both of whom had a roughly proportionate representation of ethnic minorities on their parties.

imbalance is present within the labour allocation process. Although individual criticisms could be made about each of the sources of data which have been used, the strength of the evidence lies in the consistency of the findings. The Psychology Unit at East Bridge in its study suggested three potential causative factors: a 'systematic' bias against ethnic minority groups; a genuine difference in abilities; and different preferences of ethnic minority prisoners. From the interviews which were conducted with inmates it was possible to eliminate the last suggestion because prisoners of different racial origins had similar work preferences. The second explanation (lower abilities) is also dubious. The analysis of the outside employment records of 1,255 medium-term and long-term prisoners did not indicate that those from the ethnic minorities were less able than their White counterparts.[17] Thus, credence must be given to the suggestion that racial bias lies at the root of the racial imbalance evidenced in labour allocation.

6. PRODUCING RACIAL DISCRIMINATION

Throughout this chapter evidence has been presented of the operation of racial discrimination within the prison system. These findings raise three fundamental questions: first, why does racial discrimination exist within the prison system?; second, how does it operate?; and, third, is racial discrimination a direct result of the prejudicial views of prison staff?

Clearly there are individuals within the Prison Service who are racially prejudiced and who act on these beliefs to discriminate against individual prisoners. This was particularly evident in some of the comments made by work supervisors about the under-representation, or complete absence, of ethnic minority inmates on their parties:

I wouldn't even consider having any Blacks. It's my own emotional reaction—I just wouldn't want to work with a Black. (officer supervisor)

You just can't have them doing this job. It would be different, wouldn't it, if it was a banana factory I was running here—then it would be right up their street. (civilian supervisor)

[17] See ch. 4.

Negroes are lazy . . . give a Paddy a pickaxe and he's great, give him a
sewing-machine and he's done for . . . You should give a Scot an
aggressive job . . . Negroes are lazy buggers, they like music and
leaping and dancing around . . . they have talents in other areas like in
the jungle—swinging in the trees and building mud huts. . . and they have
chips on their shoulders . . . 90 per cent of the racist feelings are on the
Negro side. (officer supervisor)

The issue which needs to be addressed, however, is how such
blatant predjudice and discrimination can continue to operate
when, under the terms of the Prison Department's race relations
policy, one of the major tasks of the Labour Boards must be to
ensure fairness of consideration in the allocation of work to all
inmates regardless of their racial origin.

First, it must be said that there was no evidence that the
Labour Boards themselves were conspiring in a policy of
discrimination. Indeed, some of them were relentless in their
efforts to stamp out any form of racially discriminatory
behaviour. However, a number of overt and covert means were
employed by supervisors which, in practice, circumvented the
formal procedures and allowed them to exercise their discretion
in the selection of their work-forces.

One of the most overt practices which was accepted and
allowed by Labour Boards was for certain 'key' work supervisors,
such as those responsible for the kitchen, mess, laundry, and
orderly positions, to pick their own men. This was variously
described as the 'old pals act' or the 'old boy network', and was
justified by officers and work supervisors on the grounds that
these areas of work were central to the smooth running of the
prison.

There were, however, a number of more subtle and covert
ways by which some supervisors avoided going through the
formal procedures. For example, at one prison a senior member
of the Labour Board described how it was common practice for
a wing cleaning supervisor who needed extra help to unlock a
prisoner of his own choice. If the inmate worked satisfactorily he
would be advised to apply for a job on the party and would be
provided with a good written reference as a proven man. The
Labour Board would then have no reasonable grounds to refuse
the application. It was claimed that one officer who was
responsible for supervising the wing cleaners had used this

device to practise racial discrimination to the extent that he had never had an ethnic minority inmate working for him.

This same member of the Labour Board also claimed that some work supervisors were able to discriminate against certain racial groups by circumventing the formal sacking procedures in order to get rid of certain men who had been placed on their party. The formal procedures dictate that before an inmate is removed from his post he should first of all be suspended, then his case should be considered by the Labour Board in the light of a written statement of the reasons for the suspension. But these work supervisors were said by this senior member of staff to use a variety of tactics to achieve their ends, such as: making unsubstantiated verbal requests to the Labour Board that inmates be removed immediately from their party; initiating disciplinary proceedings against inmates for minor transgressions which were generally accepted as 'perks' for other inmates on the party; regularly failing to unlock certain inmates on their party; and even telephoning the transfer office with a request that the unwanted inmate be transferred to another prison.

There were instances at the two other prisons also which clearly demonstrated that these methods were not confined to one institution. At one of the prisons, for example, a Black prisoner was sacked from his job in the kitchen on the grounds that he had stolen food from the stores. In effect it transpired that he was caught leaving the kitchen with a small quantity of instant coffee, which was generally recognized as a routine perk for kitchen workers and had been taken advantage of by several other members of the party with impunity. At another establishment one work supervisor used a combination of tactics to 'encourage' a Black inmate on his work-force to apply for another job. He frequently failed to call this man for work, leaving him locked in his cell and, when included in the party, he ensured that the least attractive jobs were allocated to him. The supervisor made no secret of his dislike of Black people and told White members of his work-force that if the Black prisoner did not like it, he should apply for a change of labour.

Such practices left Labour Boards, which wanted to enforce a policy of non-discrimination, with a dilemma. Clearly they could not endorse the bypassing of formal procedures, but at the same time they feared that if they became too heavy-handed in enforcing the rules, this would result in bad feeling, non-cooperation, and loss of confidence. The result could be the employment of even more underhand methods of taking on, or getting rid of, inmates from work parties. As was pointed out on more than one occasion, the reality of prison life is such that Labour Boards and work supervisors have to work together.

This is not to suggest that the Labour Boards passively accepted the attempts by works supervisors to manipulate and bypass the formal procedures. At one establishment the Labour Board together with members of the Race Relations Committee devised a plan to gather evidence against one civilian supervisor whom they suspected of acting upon unconcealed racial prejudice to discriminate against ethnic minority prisoners. He was in charge of one of the smaller workshops and had maintained an all-White work-force by sacking every Black prisoner allocated to him, on the grounds that they had failed to demonstrate either a motivation to work or an ability to master the necessary skills required for the job. In an attempt to test the validity of the supervisor's behaviour the Labour Board decided to appoint to the workshop a Black prisoner who had a high level of educational attainment, a proven record of industriousness within the prison, and who, they argued, would not provide the usual grounds for dismissal. In the event of his being sacked, the Board agreed that they would take this as evidence of discriminatory behaviour and would seek to take disciplinary proceedings against their colleague.

It would be a mistake, however, to conceive of racial discrimination in prison solely as the result of individual racial prejudice. This type of explanation is inadequate for three reasons. First, it fails to explain why individuals who may not share these views engage in racially discriminatory behaviour. Second, and conversely, it fails to acknowledge that individuals who hold racially prejudiced views may be inhibited or deterred from acting upon these beliefs. Although there is undoubtedly a connection between a person's attitudes and behaviour, this connection is by no means simplistic or mechanical. A number of factors, such as explicit social norms or severe legal sanctions, may intervene to militate against putting these prejudicial beliefs into practice. And third, explanations which rest upon individual racial prejudice alone fail to explain why institutions behave consistently over time despite changes in personnel.

This research suggests that racial discrimination is intrinsic to the social organization of prisons. In addition to being the product of a few racially prejudiced individuals, it is also the consequence of a complex interaction between racial stereo-typing and the attempts by prison staff to achieve the multifarious and sometimes conflicting goals of the institution. Most importantly it is a process which is not unique to prisons. Valerie Karn, for example, has demonstrated its application in the allocation of housing.[18] She has shown how, at times of scarce resources, building societies and local authorities are unable to meet all of their objectives and have to give priority to some over others. Karn argues that in ordering their priorities racial stereotypes are used, which systematically produce advantages for White applicants over ethnic minorities.

Prisons too have a number of competing organizational goals, including: to provide treatment and training; to keep prisoners in secure custody; to maintain good order and discipline; to treat prisoners humanely and with respect in accordance with the Prison Rules; and to provide equality of treatment to all prisoners regardless of their race. It is obvious that, in certain circumstances, these aims may be perceived as being in conflict. For example, when there are severe staff shortages, the continuance of treatment and training programmes can be regarded as jeopardizing custodial security. When this sort of conflict arises staff are required to draw up their priorities and adjust their behaviour to achieve certain goals rather than others. In line with the conclusions reached by Valerie Karn, the findings from this study demonstrate that when prison officers order their priorities, regardless of whether they are consciously expressed or unconsciously advanced, they draw upon clearly defined racial stereotypes, which systematically rationalize a certain kind of outcome, namely, the relative advantage of White prisoners and the relative disadvantage of ethnic minorities. In essence what happens is that prison staff emphasize the goals of

---

[18] V. Karn (1983), 'Race and Housing in Britain: The Role of the Major Institutions', in N. Glazer and K. Young (eds.), *Ethnic Pluralism and Public Policy* (London: Heinemann), 162–83.

good order and discipline, and management objectives associated with the efficient running of their establishments at the expense of those goals which are concerned directly with prisoners' treatment and welfare. The precise ways in which this process became apparent during the period of research can be illustrated by three examples, relating first, to the allocation of labour; second, to the promotion of inmates to positions of responsibility within the work-force; and third, to the assignment of prisoners to living accommodation.

Example One   At one establishment it emerged that over the last two years there had never been a Black inmate appointed to the prized post of receptions orderly. This was a job which required the prisoner to work closely with a small number of staff who were responsible for processing prisoners and their property when first received into the establishment, or when being discharged or transferred to other prisons. In seeking to understand how such an under-representation of Black prisoners had arisen, it became apparent that it could not be explained away by claiming that over the years all of the officers who had been responsible for this appointment held hostile attitudes towards Blacks. Repeatedly it was stated that staff chose 'the best man for the job' regardless of race. The key, however, was to be found in the qualities which were thought to constitute 'the best man'. The staff member responsible for the appointment at the time of the research argued that the job of receptions orderly required somebody who was a 'loner'; someone who could be trusted with confidential information and access to restricted property, such as money and tobacco; and someone who would not be confronted with torn loyalties if asked by other inmates to smuggle contraband through from reception. Given these criteria, he argued, it was hardly surprising that there had been an absence of Black inmates appointed. He maintained that Black prisoners rarely fell into the category of loners, they were nearly always 'hanging around in groups', and their loyalty to the Black group overrode any other responsibility. Hence, stereo-typically, a Black inmate was not seen as possessing the necessary attributes which would enable him to be identified as 'the best man' for the job.

Example Two   In another prison ethnic minority inmates were rarely, if ever, appointed to positions of responsibility in one of the large workshops, although they regularly constituted about a quarter of the work-force. The civilian supervisor explained that these positions, which were essential to the smooth running of the shop, demanded certain qualities, such as co-operation, efficiency, the ability to use initiative, and to work without supervision. Ethnic minorities, he claimed, simply did not possess these qualities.

Example Three   At four of the five establishments staff routinely dispersed Black prisoners across and within wings to ensure that the proportion of Black prisoners on any individual spur or wing did not exceed a certain limit. Their justification for this was that, typically, Black prisoners grouped together and sought to dominate wings; that White prisoners were intimidated by the presence of Black inmates in large numbers; and that inter-racial power struggles would inevitably break out unless the proportion of Black prisoners was controlled. Prison officers tended to empathize with the feelings they projected onto the White prisoners, perceiving Blacks as an invading force. In consequence, these beliefs led staff to take account of race when they were assigning accommodation to Blacks, but not when they were assigning accommodation to Whites.

The racial stereotypes which are employed in this process of discrimination need not be necessarily those of the prison officers. In some circumstances, regardless of whether the staff themselves subscribed to pejorative racial stereotypes, they were constrained by the view that if they treated Blacks and Whites equally, good order and discipline would be subverted by prejudiced and hostile Whites. Thus, at one establishment, the physical education instructor argued that it would not be in anyone's interest if he appointed an ethnic minority inmate as the gym orderly. This was because he believed that in order to preserve the more relaxed regime in the gym it was essential to have orderlies whose prestige in the inmate infrastructure enabled a degree of self-regulation and ensured that the facilities were not abused. He believed that, in general, Black prisoners did not command this level of peer respect and that in his prison the dominant White group would not accept an ethnic minority prisoner in this role. At another establishment there had never been a Black inmate assigned to the task of wing orderly because, in the words of the officer responsible, 'I don't want a riot on my hands . . . this job involves handling food and picking up rations . . . the man in this position has to be accepted and trusted by staff and inmates alike.' And at another establishment both the officer in charge of receptions and the laundry officer said that they had not employed any Black inmates because they anticipated that the objections of White prisoners to work along side the Blacks would create too much tension.

What these examples illustrate is how racial stereotypes are used by prison staff to justify and rationalize the belief that it is only possible to go so far in pursuing the goal of fairness and equality before a conflict arises with the goals of maintaining good order or organizational efficiency. In choosing to give priority to the latter, they reinforce the advantage of the White majority to the relative disadvantage of ethnic minority inmates.

6

The Stumbling-Blocks

A clear intention of the Prison Department's race relations policy is to set standards of professional conduct amongst prison staff. It is not a device which has been specifically designed to change people's attitudes but a means to effect certain changes in their behaviour at work. The findings from this research clearly indicate that changes are required if racial discrimination is to be eliminated in the Prison Service. During the course of the study, however, it became apparent that there were a number of stumbling-blocks, which seriously hindered the implementation of the policy. The purpose of this chapter is to identify these obstacles. The first is associated with the drafting of the policy statement itself. It will be argued that there is a lack of clarity and precision in *what* prison staff are being asked to do and, in particular, *why* they are being asked to do it. Second, there are problems associated with the adequacy and effectiveness of those measures which have been designed to promote the achievement and enforcement of the policy directives. Third, there is a notable absence of specific mechanisms to sanction unprofessional conduct in this area. Finally, it will be suggested that there are features currently inherent in the social organization of prisons which help to perpetuate the processes by which racial discrimination is produced and which are, therefore, in direct conflict with the successful development of the department's race relations policy.

1. POLICY CLARIFICATION

The Prison Department's race relations policy has been demonstrably capable of stirring powerful feelings amongst staff. Yet the Prison Service is no stranger to issues which require delicate and diplomatic handling. The provision of Mother and Baby Units; coping with roof-top protests; and the care of the mentally disordered are all sensitive subjects which have confronted the department and which have caused controversy and fervent debate both inside and outside the Prison Service. The question for policy-makers is whether there is anything special about a race relations policy which distinguishes it from other kinds of programmes and which has implications for its formulation, reception, and implementation on the ground. This research suggests that one crucial and distinctive feature of the Prison Department's race relations policy is that it issues directives about personal conduct which are not related exclusively to an individual's job but pertain to, and make implicit judgments about, the behaviour of members of staff outside the prison walls. Most policies and training within the Prison Service inform staff about specific procedures and communicate skills which relate directly to particular prison tasks and about which individuals are not expected to have prior expertise or knowledge. Examples of this are policies relating to the categorization and allocation of prisoners, the restraint of violent inmates, and the parole system. Instructions on race relations, whilst directed toward the professional conduct of prison staff, inevitably call into question general attitudes, which may be perceived as matters for individual moral judgment and personal social skills.

The significance of this is borne out by the ways in which officers in this study variously responded to particular parts of the policy statement. Those areas concerned with the provision of specific religious and dietary facilities for ethnic minorities were not imbued with controversy but overwhelmingly accepted as a legitimate part of the job and a relevant component of training. On the other hand, sections of the policy which gave directions to officers about their inter-personal behaviour created considerable resentment. The issues were perceived to relate not only to professional expertise but also to private conduct and, as a result, staff questioned the relevance of such training, claiming that they were already competent in these respects. Indeed the appropriateness of issuing policy in this area at all was doubted. The comment made on many occasions was that it was absurd to try to legislate for people to like each other.

Apart from the inherent sensitivity of the department's policy, it is also dealing with a subject of considerable complexity, which does not lend itself easily to clear-cut directives. The stated intention of the policy is to produce equality of treatment and opportunity for all inmates regardless of their race. The current statement gives explicit advice and instructions on certain strategies designed to achieve this aim, such as the avoidance of derogatory language and the provision of religious and dietary facilities. In other respects, however, the guidance given in the statement raises more questions than it answers. This is particularly evident in the advice given to governors concerning the avoidance of segregation and separation. To this end governors are encouraged to ensure that in all contexts inmates of different races are represented in proportion to their numbers in the establishment. In addition, they are urged to discourage prisoners from choosing to perpetuate imbalance and actively to prevent 'self-discrimination' where it places 'racial constraint' upon the availability of facilities and activities. In essence what is propounded is the dispersal of Black and Asian prisoners within the majority population. Significantly, this guidance is seen to apply to all establishments, regardless of the size of their ethnic minority populations, because they 'all ... share (currently or potentially) the same problems and challenges'.[1]

Important consequences flow from this, which are not directly addressed in the policy statement and which create grey areas both in practice and in theory. The practice of dispersing racial groups is justified in the department's statement on the grounds of ensuring equality of opportunity in prison. At the same time, however, such a policy may actually threaten the safety, security, and decency of individual prisoners. If, for example, inmates are required to share cells against their will with individuals who have strong racist views, or with those whose customs and practices are very different from their own, this could lead to victimization and/or be construed as constituting extra punishment. Currently different practices operate, even within the same establishment, to deal with this problem. At one prison an active member of the National Front refused to share a cell with a Black inmate. The senior officer informed him that, contrary

[1] Home Office (1983), Prison Department Circular Instruction 56/1983, para. 10.

to opinions expressed in the popular press, he was not staying at the Ritz and that he could not pick and choose the colour of his cellmate. The prisoner refused to accept this decision and was subsequently charged with a disciplinary offence and provided with alternative accommodation in the segregation unit. In the same establishment another officer anticipated racial dislike when allocating cells and, whenever possible, allowed prisoners to share accommodation with men of their own race. Clearly the question arises whether there are any legitimate reasons for prisoners to choose to be racially separate and, if there are, whether the consequences flowing from the exercise of this choice are acceptable and tolerable within the prison context.

A further dilemma arises if ethnic minority prisoners are to be proportionately distributed in prison activities such as work and training. The difficulty is that this potentially limits their opportunities to gain access to particular jobs and courses, as well as to associate and work with people of their own race. The problem is exacerbated in establishments with a very low proportion of ethnic minorities. If, for example, 5 per cent of the population are Black then, in theory, each Black prisoner has less opportunity of gaining his preferred option than in an establishment where 40 per cent are Black. Inevitably the implementation of the policy has different consequences in different establishments. Establishments do not, in other words, 'all . . . share . . . the same problems and challenges'. It will almost certainly be argued that, in practice, this kind of violation of equal treatment and opportunity would not arise because the rules of common sense would prevail. But what are the rules of common sense? Are there levels of populations within which a policy of proportional distribution should not be operated? And, if so, is it a matter for individual discretion?

If these grey areas are to be given any clarity, a prior question has to be answered, namely, what purposes are served by racial dispersal in prisons? Three objectives present themselves: first, to ensure equality of treatment and opportunity; second, to foster harmonious relations amongst a multi-racial inmate population; and third, to control racial grouping amongst ethnic minorities and thus reduce the threat of conflict between well-entrenched racial factions. If equality of opportunity is the sole objective of racial dispersal then clearly it is not necessary to enforce a proportional distribution of racial groups in all environments of the prison. Only those areas which afford an opportunity to exercise discrimination require control of this kind. Consequently those situations in which self-separation does not imply the giving of undue advantage, such as in the allocation of identical living accommodation, would not warrant racial dispersal. In addition if equality of treatment and opportunity were to be achieved it would be necessary, especially in establishments with very low numbers of ethnic minority prisoners, to suspend the practice of proportional distribution altogether and employ other methods for identifying and tackling discrimination.

Equality of opportunity is not, however, the only purpose served by racial dispersal. If the Prison Department wishes to encourage closer communication and interaction between racial groups then arguments could be made both for and against the adoption of a policy of racial dispersal. Whether it is an effective or counter-productive measure in achieving this end, however, is dependent, at least in part, upon the extent to which it is supported by other integrative practices. Clearly if the aim is to foster racial integration as opposed to preventing racial segregation then a policy of dispersal would require the accompaniment of other measures designed to promote and control the development of specific types of attitude and behaviour.

The reduction of potential and actual conflict between well-entrenched racial groups is the third objective and this could well be served by enforcing the dispersal of ethnic minorities in all prison settings. Certainly this was stated as the primary objective of dispersing Black prisoners across wings at Littlebourne. The effectiveness of such a measure, however, would be dependent upon the relative numbers of racial minorities in any given prison population. Obviously the higher the proportion of minorities the less likely it would be to inhibit effectively the possibility of racial grouping. Thus, different strategies would be required in prisons with different populations. Alternatively a system of 'busing' could be introduced to limit the numbers of ethnic minorities in any one establishment. Although this practice is not official policy, it is known to have occurred in some prisons where the numbers of Black prisoners were deemed to be in excess of the capability of the establishment. It was claimed that such procedures were not racist because they were not designed or used solely to control the numbers of Blacks, but to restrict the numbers of any particular group which could present a threat to good order and discipline. Hence it was argued that similar practices had been used to limit the numbers of Londoners, drug abusers, and sex offenders. In addition it was suggested that confining the proportion of Black prisoners in any one prison markedly improved the state of race relations because White inmates did not feel threatened and were thus able to accept the Blacks who were allocated there.

It could be argued that all three of the above options are valid and justifiable goals for the Prison Department to pursue and, indeed, are implied to a greater or lesser degree in the policy statement. Each, however, has different practical and ethical implications for the dispersal of ethnic minority prisoners and makes different demands upon staff. The dual approach to race relations, which both promotes equality of opportunity and controls the numbers of ethnic minorities in any given setting, is characteristic of the strategies used by British Governments in successive Race Relations and Immigration Acts and of the Prison Department's policy on race relations. It is, however, an approach which is imbued with contradictions. A policy based upon equality of opportunity assumes that the Black minority are part of the community and are here to stay. It presumes that the threat to law and order, or good order and discipline, comes from denying racial minorities the protection of equal rights. Immigration control has also been seen as an important mechanism for the promotion of racial harmony; the assumption being that one of the greatest threats to racial tolerance is the uncontrolled number of Black immigrants entering Britain.[2] Yet conversely, it has been argued that a policy based upon the control of numbers implicitly fails to recognize the Black minority as an equal part of the community and ignores the potentially negative consequences which such controls have for those Black people already present.[3] Instead it has been suggested that 'the numbers game' designates Black people as a group which can be tolerated only within certain limits and that,

[2] M. D. A. Freeman and S. Spencer (1979), 'The State, the Law and Race Relations in Britain Today', *Current Legal Problems*, 32: 117–42.
[3] Ibid. 127.

beyond this, their presence *per se* is undesirable.[4] MacDonald has argued that, within the context of maintaining law and order or good order discipline, a policy based upon the control of numbers assumes that Black people signify disruption simply by being present in any given situation.[5]

Clearly policy cannot legislate for every eventuality but is intended to provide guidelines within which individual prisons must work. Some open-endedness is, therefore, inevitable and even desirable, enabling the development of tailor-made strategies for each establishment. The grey areas which have been outlined here, however, do not fall into this category since they do not concern the nuts and bolts of specific initiatives but relate to fundamental questions about the purposes and goals of departmental policy. Lack of clarity in these areas creates confusion and provides opportunities for divergent and anomalous practices both within and between establishments.

2. COMMUNICATION AND ENFORCEMENT OF POLICY

The success of a race relations policy in prisons relies not only upon the perspicuity and directness of its goals but also upon the effectiveness of the strategies which have been designed to communicate and enforce them. Currently these measures fall into three main categories: education and training; management strategies; and monitoring. The department also seeks to recruit more staff from ethnic minority communities as an essential part of its commitment to good race relations. But this research raised questions about the adequacy of these mechanisms and the extent to which they have been effective in achieving the aims of the policy.

(i) Recruitment

The recruitment of ethnic minority staff is regarded by the Prison Department as an important strategy in promoting both

---

[4] Ibid.

[5] I. A. MacDonald (1977), *Race Relations—The New Law* (London: Butterworths), 8.

good race relations within prisons and equality of opportunity in the employment of staff. To achieve this end specially targeted recruitment drives have been initiated to encourage more Black and Asian people to join the Prison Service and a culturally unbiased test has been designed to ensure that all applicants are treated equally and impartially, regardless of race or ethnicity. But to date there has been a notable lack of success in recruiting ethnic minorities. Indeed, they currently represent less than 1 per cent of prison staff. Reliable data are required to understand why recruitment campaigns have had so little impact. It is unclear why so few Black and Asian people apply to join the Prison Service; whether those who do apply are disproportionately failing to be selected and, if so, for what reason; and the extent to which they are over-represented amongst those who withdraw because they are discouraged by the processes of selection and training.

The development of a culturally unbiased qualifying test is clearly an essential prerequisite for the promotion of equality of opportunity in the appointment of prison staff. But if recruitment procedures are to promote the department's race relations policy it raises the issue of whether they should be doing more than simply attracting Black and Asian people into the Prison Service. For example, should recruitment panels screen out candidates whose views about race relations are so diametrically opposed to those enshrined in the official policy that they indicate an inflexible attitude? It may, of course, be argued that the existing policy is not designed to change attitudes but to control behaviour. Nevertheless if a central plank of the training platform is that racial prejudice must be challenged and that staff must understand the relevance of race relations to their work, then, on the basis of these criteria, it could be seen as a rational development for the Prison Service to ensure that those recruited are not hostile and resistant to the principles underlying the department's policy. The crucial question is whether recruitment procedures should be developed which would include some means of discerning how applicants regard issues of racial equality and discrimination, and whether racial bigotry should be used as grounds for exclusion from the Prison Service.

(ii) Strategies for Education and Training

The importance attached by the Prison Department to good race relations is often claimed to be proven by the fact that at a time of considerable financial restraint and severe cuts in training budgets national race relations courses have been maintained at their former level.

The linchpin of national training is the recently established 'generic' course at which teams from each prison are required to draw up action plans which they are expected to implement on their return to the establishment.[6] Typically, the action plans cover a wide range of objectives, such as the review of library facilities for ethnic minority inmates, the elimination of racial stereotyping from written reports, and the development of links with outside organizations such as the Community Relations Council. However, many staff were not aware when they embarked upon the training that they would be required to act as part of a team. They expressed concern that considerable logistical difficulties would be faced in scheduling regular meetings which all members of the team would be able to attend. Some of the participants suggested that, had they known that the course required the setting up of a race relations team, different personnel would have been chosen. The effectiveness of the team approach was further undermined by the fact that some of the staff who had been sent on the course were shortly to retire from the Prison Service, or were to be transferred to another establishment. It was also apparent that certain members of staff had been selected because someone in their home establishment had thought it would 'do him good'. These conscripts were officers who held particularly sceptical views about the relevance of race relations and for whom such training was solely an opportunity for exploring their own deeply in-grained views and opinions. Clearly a primary condition for the effectiveness of generic training is the dissemination of clear criteria governing the selection of team members are fully prerequisite is that governors and training officers are fully aware that they are sending a staff *team* and that their choice of

---

[6] The structure and nature of these courses are described in ch. 2.

team members takes account of the feasibility of these individuals operating as a group upon their return.

The dictum that race relations is the responsibility of all members of staff is undoubtedly reinforced by the team approach inherent in generic training. But do the training programmes go far enough in emphasizing this message? Currently no particular guidance is given to staff about the importance of race in exercising their discretion when carrying out such duties as reception, induction, classification and transfer, cell allocation, or labour allocation. Training courses could also be established for work supervisors and for members of Boards of Visitors and independent members of Local Review Committees.[7] Clearly a race relations dimension would not be relevant to every aspect of staff training, but the question is whether the emphasis should be placed upon justifying the exclusion of such training rather than having to make a case for its inclusion.

Until recently a striking omission in the organization of generic training was the lack of any systematic follow-up to discover how far the action plans had been implemented in the individual establishments. This has now been rectified by the Prison Service College, which has conducted a survey to assess the effectiveness of the programme and to identify areas for change. The dilemma is whether this should be an isolated exercise or repeated on a regular basis. The answer to this is contingent upon identifying what purposes the data could serve and who should be the recipients of such information. Regularly collecting survey material and feeding it back into the system may assist the implementation of policy in three main ways. First, it could provide essential knowledge upon which those who plan and conduct training programmes can review and develop their approach and methods. Second, by bringing together the experiences of a wide range of institutions, it may enable common problems to be identified and good practices to be promoted. Third, it could establish a means of ensuring that training is taken seriously and that the plans developed do not remain mere paper exercises. If each survey were to include not only those establishments which had sent teams to be trained

---

[7] An optional training module already exists for members of Boards of Visitors.

during the current year but also those which sent teams in previous years a continuous record could be kept of the progress of individual prisons. The introduction of a longitudinal element could also be used in assessing the practicality of a team approach to training. It would enable account to be taken of such functional exigencies as staff promotions and transfers and the facilities available for training replacements to a team.

Such a programme would fit neatly into the new system of management accountability for race relations. It places a responsibility upon governors to implement action plans; upon regional offices to ensure that information is disseminated and that establishments with particular problems are given expert assistance; upon P3 and the Regional Race Relations Co-ordinators Group to confront issues of general policy significance and to formulate specific guidance on problems commonly shared by establishments; and upon the Prisons Board to ensure that the Prison Service is furnished with sufficient resources to maintain and develop training programmes and to implement the initiatives which they generate.

(iii) Strategies for Effective Management

During the first phase of this research two central problems were identified for the administration of the Prison Department's race relations policy. The first was the inconsistency with which the policy was being implemented at both regional and establishment levels; and the second concerned the difficulties of communication between headquarters, regional offices and individual establishments.

The availability of local race relations training, for example, varied across different regions and appeared to be contingent upon the size of the training budget, the availability of staff to attend courses, and the priority attached to race relations training. Ironically information provided by the regional race relations co-ordinators revealed that those regions accommodating the highest numbers of ethnic minority prisoners had less training opportunities than those with smaller populations. Differences also occurred in the nature and extent of communication between regional co-ordinators and race relations liaison officers within individual establishments. Although guidelines had been circulated on the role of the race relations liaison officers, there remained in practice considerable diversity, which tended to reflect differing levels of personal motivations and encouragement from superiors, rather than specific institutional needs. This was particularly apparent in the extent to which race relations liaison officers developed contacts with outside community organizations and in their approaches to ethnic monitoring.

The second set of problems were associated with blockages in channels of communication, which seriously inhibited the ability of individuals to carry out duties alloted to them. The role of the regional co-ordinators, for example, was hindered by the lack of a system of direct contact with the majority of establishments in their region. Gaining information about race relations at other establishments was therefore dependent upon informal communication and *ad hoc* arrangements. Similarly P3 (which occupies a pivotal position in monitoring the state of race relations generally, drafting policy statements and disseminating information) received only partial and incomplete feedback from regions and individual establishments. Most significantly the processes of communication ensured that there was no single focal point to collate race relations complaints and no record of the total number of such complaints made in each year. Although P3 received complaints filed by sentenced adult male prisoners, another division in headquarters dealt with complaints from women and young offenders, another with those from life sentenced prisoners, and another with complaints from those held on remand.

The publication of the latest Circular Instruction, in November 1986, set in motion a series of organizational changes which confront a number of these problems. Systems of communication between the different levels of the bureaucracy have now been formalized and procedures for feedback from establishments and lines of accountability have been clearly spelt out. Inconsistency across regions has also been reduced over the last two years by the development of the Regional Race Relations Co-ordinators Group, which has involved the regional co-ordinators in a system of corporate planning on race relations.[8] In addition

[8] See ch. 2 for details on the composition of the Regional Race Relations Co-ordinators Group.

an attempt has been made to standardize the methods by which the state of race relations is assessed in individual establishments. A check-list has been circulated, which consists of thirteen key questions relating not only to the provision of specific facilities for ethnic minorities but also to inter-personal conduct between inmates and between inmates and staff. Information is called for on discriminatory behaviour by staff, such as in the use of derogatory language, jokes, or the display of cartoons. Details are also requested about incidents occurring between inmates of different ethnic origins which have been perceived, either by those involved or by staff, to have been contributed to, or caused by, racial differences. Most of the information required, however, is dependent upon efficient and consistent systems of monitoring.

(iv) Procedures for Monitoring

The achievement of non-discriminatory regimes hinges to a large degree upon the effectiveness of monitoring. The check-list identifies a range of areas in which the ethnic mix of the population should be reviewed: namely, units of accommodation, including the hospital or medical wing; work parties; education and vocational training; pre-release schemes; sporting activities; and sick parades. In addition it calls for information about the representation of ethnic minority groups amongst those who are the subject of minor wing reports, or who appear on governors and Boards of Visitors adjudications, as well as those who are on Rule 43 or on punishment in the segregation unit.[9] It is too soon to know whether monitoring in all of these areas is being carried out effectively since the check-list was issued after the completion of the field-work for this research. Nevertheless the study has identified a number of stumbling-blocks in the collection of reliable data. Most of the difficulties arise from the lack of clear instructions on how establishments should set about gathering and compiling this statistical information. For example, there has been no guidance about the frequency with which monitoring should be carried out, the ethnic codes to be

[9] This includes adult prisoners segregated on Rule 43 for reasons of good order and discipline (Rule 46 in young offender establishments) and those who have sought Rule 43 (46) for their own protection.

used, or whether all the specified activities and facilities should be monitored in the same way.

Indeed, it has to be questioned whether it is desirable and appropriate for there to be standardized practices for all types and sizes of establishment. The introduction of such guidelines would, of course, presuppose a clearly defined objective. Currently it is not made explicit whether the monitoring required by the check-list is intended only as a tool for internal management, or whether it is to be collated at a national level and used for comparative purposes. One function which the compilation of national statistical data could serve is to provide an empirical basis to challenge some of the deeply entrenched stereotypes. For example, a view in one establishment that Black prisoners disliked certain jobs and that 'it's impossible to get them to work in certain areas', could be usefully reassessed in the light of what is happening in other establishments. Similarly in the area of disciplinary offences, a national breakdown of information would provide a valuable tool to assess current practices within individual establishments.

The only area in which specific guidance has been issued on ethnic monitoring is in the coding of inmates on their reception into prison. Yet during the course of the research these procedures were still being carried out inconsistently across different establishments. At one prison, for example, the officer in charge of coding new receptions refused to acknowledge that there was a range of Indo-Asian categories and stalwartly categorized all prisoners who looked as if their origins might have been in the Indian sub-continent as Pakistani. At the same prison the race relations liaison officer monitored the numbers of ethnic minorities in certain work tasks by assessing the race of an inmate from his appearance in his photograph. His system of colour-coding for prisoners of mixed race resulted in a number of inmates of mixed West Indian and European origin being coded into one of the Indo-Asian categories because the colour of their skin was thought to match most closely that of Indian and Pakistani prisoners. At another prison no monitoring of work was undertaken at all.

The research also revealed that even when monitoring procedures were being properly and rigorously employed the scope of the data was not sufficient to identify the more subtle practices of discrimination. At best establishments were maintaining records of the numbers of inmates of different racial groups employed in different parts of the prison. But no account was taken of the ways in which inmates were treated within specific areas of work and training. For example, a serious omission was the lack of any monitoring of the length of time that inmates remained in a particular job. There was also no monitoring of the representation of ethnic minorities amongst those in positions of responsibility within specific work parties. In the kitchens, for instance, there is a clear division of labour, with sweeping-up and washing-up at one end of the spectrum, and food preparation and cooking at the other. Certainly the supervisor in one kitchen stated that very few Black inmates ever progressed beyond the most menial tasks. In the outside work parties, too, similar divisions may be found.

If the purpose of monitoring work allocation and other activities in the prison is to combat racial discrimination then procedures are required which are sensitive to the less obvious as well as to the more manifest forms of discriminatory behaviour. But during the course of the research warnings were issued against the development of more rigorous systems. First, it was claimed that more sophisticated monitoring procedures would require a greater input of staff time. Second, in establishments where there is a rapid throughput of inmates, it was said to be virtually impossible to maintain detailed monitoring. Finally, it was feared that the process of collecting the necessary information could result in a very high degree of resentment by prison staff, who might object to their professional conduct being policed in this way.

Despite the efforts of individual race relations liaison officers to introduce a system of monitoring and personally to challenge racial prejudice and discrimination, they were inevitably labouring under a number of structural disadvantages. The job appeared to have very few rewards: no specific time had been allocated for the duties they were expected to perform; there was little prestige attached to their tasks; and they were given no special authority within the prison. The job of monitoring the professional conduct of one's colleagues can hardly be popular, especially in an occupational culture as closely knit as that of prison officers.

A final question to be addressed if ethnic monitoring in prisons is to achieve its goal is whether there should be some independent scrutiny of the procedures and results. The research was particularly concerned to look at how Boards of Visitors, as the independent 'watch-dogs', perceived their role *vis-à-vis* the department's race relations policy. Members of the Boards of Visitors at all five establishments were asked if they thought they should routinely receive the results of the monitoring relating to the various jobs and training courses and to the representation of ethnic minorities amongst those subject to disciplinary proceedings. None of them thought they should receive this information as a matter of routine. Instead a general suspicion of statistics was expressed and they said that they would much rather rely on their own observations and 'feel' of the establishment. Also some of them felt that such information was essentially for prison managers and that if the governor already received these statistics the matter would most probably be in hand. In general, board members were unable to recall any specific race relations complaints made by inmates and this was taken by all of those who were interviewed to indicate an absence of race relations problems in their establishment.

At one establishment the Board of Visitors was not aware of the results of monitoring which had shown that inmates of West Indian origin were significantly more likely than any other group to be unemployed or to be allocated to what were regarded as the least attractive jobs in the prison. When asked whether this was the sort of information in which they should be expected to take an active interest their responses were hedged with qualifications. All but one of the members believed that they should not become involved unless the statistics could be shown to *prove* that the allocation of work was the *direct* result of racial discrimination. Some went on to say that they very much doubted that this was so because jobs were allocated to whichever inmate was the most suitable. As they saw it the probability was that the West Indians concerned were unemployed outside, or had very poor work records. Under these circumstances, they maintained, it was hardly surprising to find them in the least attractive jobs in prison.

3. THE ABSENCE OF EFFECTIVE SANCTIONS

It follows from what has been said so far that there are major obstacles, both in theory and in practice, which inhibit the effectiveness of those measures which have been designed to promote racial equality in prisons. But in addition to the problems pertaining to existing measures there are important mechanisms of enforcement which are missing altogether. A significant omission is that there are no separate or clearly defined procedures through which an inmate who feels that he or she has suffered racial discrimination can make a complaint. The majority of race relations liaison officers did not publicize to inmates that they held this position and did not see themselves as vehicles for complaints. Indeed, their job description does not require them to take on this responsibility. But an exception to this was found at Newfield youth custody centre. Here a local policy statement had been issued by the governor, endorsed by the Prison Officers Association and circulated to both staff and inmates, which made provision for inmates to bring any complaint of racial discrimination to the race relations liaison officer.

In general, it was argued that formal procedures were unnecessary because prisoners were already protected by the 1976 Race Relations Act. Ironically the validity of this statement was only confirmed after the Prison Department had contested the principle in the case of the *Prison Department* v. *Alexander*, by arguing that the 1976 Act did not apply to the provision of facilities in prison. Furthermore, although it was found that a complaint was permissible under the provisions of the Act, in this instance the decision does not constitute a legal precedent because it was made in the County Court.[10]

But putting to one side questions about the extent of the department's liability, there are also practical factors, in addition to the general problems outlined in Chapters 1 and 5, which make it difficult for prison inmates to gain advantage from the protections and remedies afforded by this legislation. Of central significance is the factor of time. There would seem to be little

---

[10] See ch. 1 for further discussion of this case.

incentive for the majority of prisoners serving relatively short sentences to issue a complaint when the necessary legal remedies would take longer to achieve than the duration of their sentence.

The nature of the remedies available are also of questionable relevance, particularly for those already discharged at the time of the hearing. Three specific disposals are available to a tribunal or court. They may issue an order declaring the rights of the parties. In addition a court may issue an injunction or order to a particular person or organization 'to perform or not to commit, or to cease committing specified acts'. Tribunals in employment cases may also make a recommendation (but it is only a recommendation) that the respondent take a particular course of action, such as re-employing or promoting the complainant. Finally, a tribunal or court may require the respondent to pay the complainant compensation or damages, the amount being based upon the direct financial loss sustained by the complainant, such as loss of earnings, and upon an estimate of other less precisely calculable damages, such as injured feelings.

The fact that an inmate may well have to come into daily contact with the respondents to his complaint in what is an already unequal relationship suggests that a remedy which simply restates his rights would be unlikely to encourage him to risk creating an atmosphere of acrimony which could affect a whole range of his activities. Alternatively a court injunction which might, for example, enable a prisoner to be promoted to a particular job in the kitchen would hardly be an attractive option to someone already released from the system, or relevant to someone transferred to another establishment. The provision of financial compensation to complainant prisoners could be seen as an appropriate remedy. But if this is to be based upon prison wages it again becomes an irrelevance to those already discharged from prison and is only likely to be practically meaningful to inmates serving long sentences and thus rooted within the prison labour economy.

Finally, there remains a conspicuous absence of specific sanctions against those whose behaviour in dealing with racial minorities in prison contravenes the directives of the department's policy. Some prison governors and senior administrators in the Prison Department were not opposed, in principle, to the introduction of sanctions similar to those which now regulate the conduct of the police. But they questioned the practical value of such measures. It was suggested that the problem was not a lack of proper procedures since the existing Code of Discipline adequately provides for all breaches of prison discipline by staff. The major stumbling-block was considered to be the evaluation of evidence and standards of proof. As one prison governor put it, 'We already have the teeth to combat racism, we know it goes on but we just can't prove it.' In general the symbolic value of introducing sanctions was not disputed. But again, in practice, it was feared that such measures would be interpreted by prison officers as heavy-handed and, in consequence, would succeed only in arousing resentment and hostility towards the policy.

4. ORGANIZATIONAL STUMBLING-BLOCKS

A frontline defence of racial discrimination in prisons is the argument that prisons simply reflect what is going on in society at large. In other words, it is inevitable, even if undesirable, for there to be racial prejudice and racial discrimination in prisons, because that is precisely what is happening in the outside world. The implication of these statements is clear: racial discrimination is a normal part of social life and thus a normal part of prison life. In consequence, the Prison Department can only be expected to go so far in achieving racial equality because the cause (and thus the cure) has to be found beyond the prison walls.

But to depict the social world of the prison simply as a microcosm of society is to deny the special characteristics of such institutions and to overlook the consequences which these have for race relations. If the processes of discrimination described in the previous chapter are to be effectively tackled two questions have to be answered. First, why is it that internal discipline and organizational efficiency have been granted such high priority at the expense of other regime goals? And second, why is it that such specific racial stereotypes are so pervasive amongst the uniformed staff?

This research suggests that there is an interrelationship between specific features of the occupational culture of prison officers and the organization of prison regimes which throws some light on these issues. Together they produce a number of structural dilemmas which are unique to the Prison Service in combating racial discrimination. In describing the relevant features of the occupational culture of prison officers there is an inevitable danger that what emerges becomes interpreted as nothing more than a crude form of stereotyping. There is, however, a distinction to be drawn between a stereotype and a valid generalization. A stereotype in this context essentially distorts reality. It is a value-laden concept, which incorporates invidious and pejorative depictions. A valid generalization, on the other hand, is rooted within empirical evidence and renders clarification and authenticity without moral evaluation.

The prison officer culture—that is, the values, norms, and rules which inform their conduct—is not monolithic, universal or unchanging. Nevertheless, as an occupational group, prison officers face common problems in carrying out the role they are mandated to perform and, in consequence, it is not surprising that a level of conformity in outlook may be discerned. Inevitably any discussion about the roles of prison officers must take into account the wide range of establishments encompassed within the system. At one end of the scale, high-security prisons for professional criminals, at the other, local prisons providing 'a warm if rather spartan refuge for homeless, rootless alcoholics'.[11] Nevertheless it is a valid generalization that prison officers have developed a patterned set of understandings which help them to cope with, and adjust to, the pressures and tensions which confront them.

This study suggests that in all types of establishment the intrinsic conditions of a prison officer's work facilitate and encourage the stereotyping of prisoners. Clearly this is not limited to racial stereotypes but includes the stereotyping of a wide range of inmate groups, such as terrorist prisoners, sex offenders, youth custody trainees, and many others. One of the reasons that stereotyping has become particularly functional for prison officers is that their work has been characterized within the occupational culture by three interdependent features:

[11] V. Stern (1987), *Bricks of Shame* (Harmondsworth: Penguin), 59.

namely authority, suspicion, and danger. Throughout their training they are taught to maintain their authority in all situations over an unconsenting population; to be constantly vigilant of that population, who, they are warned, will take any opportunity to challenge their authority; and, in consequence, to be ever aware of the potential danger in which they work. Within this context stereotyping becomes a means by which prison officers attempt to order their environment and predict the behaviour of others so that they can achieve their goals of ensuring security and safety, good order and discipline.

But racial stereotyping is not only encouraged by the ways in which a prison officer's role is defined it is also reinforced by the social context in which he lives and works. It is a milieu characterized by conditions which inevitably create a degree of social isolation and internal solidarity. Shift work and the problem of 'switching off' from the highly charged atmosphere of the job create a situation in which much off-duty socializing occurs with others who work in the Prison Service. The opportunity to move anywhere in the country during the course of their career and the probability of transfer following promotion also contribute to their dependence upon the Prison Service for their social contacts. Communal identity has been further reinforced by the tendency for many prison officers, and especially those working in isolated establishments, to live in Prison Service accommodation situated in discrete housing estates. The provision of staff clubs attached to each prison also encourages officers and their families to mix socially. Since very few prison officers are members of ethnic minority groups social relations with Black and Asian people are generally limited to their interactions with inmates.

Internal solidarity is also a feature of their working environment. Whilst this is closely linked with the social isolation of prison officers, it is also a product of the intrinsic conditions of their job and the consequent need to be able to rely on colleagues in a tight spot. Indeed, officers routinely claimed that, when on duty, there was little they would not do for a fellow officer because 'one day you may have to depend on him for your very life'. As in every organization, inter-personal conflicts exist but these detract little from the 'them and us' outlook characteristic of the officer subculture. Within this perspective, however, distinctions are made between different types of 'them'.

One type of 'them' exists in the ivory towers of head office. These are the civil servants who, it is said, manage the system from a distance and who have no real grasp of what it is like at the sharp end of the market. The isolation and solidarity of the occupational culture of prison officers is inevitably shaped by the history of dispute and confrontation which has characterized industrial relations in the Prison Service over the last two decades. From a recent survey of staff attitudes and from interviews conducted during the course of this research it was apparent that amongst prison officers there is a strong sense of being undervalued by their employers.[12] They expressed the view that management did not care enough about prison staff; that officers were not supported when criticized; and that the department was frightened of public opinion. Most importantly they felt let down by Home Office officials, believing that successive waves of ministers and civil servants had been dishonest and manipulative in their negotiations with prison officers. But in addition to this, the Office of Population Censuses and Surveys study showed that prison officers also felt a degree of trepidation in their relationships with the outside world.[13] Nearly half of those interviewed said that they preferred not to tell people what they did for a living. Outsiders were thought to be suspicious and guarded once they knew they were prison officers and a large minority felt that people looked down on them because of their job. In essence it was concluded that officers' views of their own occupation were generally jaundiced.

But it would be misleading and inaccurate to suggest that prison officers' interpretations of social situations are entirely constructed from their social contacts within the Prison Service. Inevitably their view of the world is built up and reinforced throughout their wider social experience. It would not, therefore, be unreasonable to expect that prison officers share many of the values of the social groups from which they are drawn. According to the Office of Population Censuses and Surveys study most of them are middle-aged family men whose

---

[12] Office of Population Censuses and Surveys (1985), *Staff Attitudes in the Prison Service* (London: HMSO), 50.   [13] Ibid. 62.

educational and employment backgrounds are typical of manual workers. Their social backgrounds, however, indicate a conservative orientation. The uniformed section of the Prison Service is constituted as a hierarchical highly disciplined organization and many prison officers have had previous experience of other uniformed jobs. At a time when a military background is becoming increasingly rare as many as 51 per cent of discipline officers currently employed by the Prison Service had previously served in the armed forces and most of these (78 per cent) were volunteer regulars and not National Servicemen.[14] The study suggests that for these men work in the ranks of the Prison Service may provide a secure and well-ordered working environment typically absent in civilian life. Moreover, having joined the Prison Service, many appear to make it their life's work. Even basic grade discipline officers share between them an average of ten years' service and the average for chief officers is nearly thirty years.

Within this context it is quite possible that the negative stereotypes which officers apply to Black inmates reflect attitudes and beliefs which are held by members of outside society. But the isolation, solidarity, and homogeneity of the prison officer culture, together with the lack of input from ethnic minority officers, provide ideal conditions for the reinforcement of such stereotyping. As the Office of Population Censuses and Surveys study concluded:

Socially, prison officers are a remarkably homogeneous group of people ... they work together for exceedingly long hours in a disciplined environment in a way that binds them together as part of a distinct community ... The prison officer's involvement with the prison he serves appears, viewed objectively, to be scarcely less than that of his clients ... Overall, they share a social homogeneity that makes it easy for them to act together.[15]

There is, however, one further area of the occupational culture which has implications for the development of a race relations policy in prisons: namely, the officers' sense of professionalism. This has a bearing not upon the social process of stereotyping but upon the ways in which priority and importance are attached to certain organizational goals over others.

[14] Ibid. 19.   [15] Ibid. 22.

A primary aim in the management of any prison is maintaining the security and safety of staff and prisoners. But what has to be questioned is how security is defined and how it is pursued. Prison discipline and organizational efficiency are not necessarily synonymous with prison security. Similarly conflict in these areas does not necessarily represent a threat to conditions of safe custody. It is well known throughout the Prison Service that security does not rest solely upon locks, bolts, and bars, 'If activity is planned around the individual, and relies on, and promotes the relationships between individuals, it enhances the security and safety of the establishments.'[16] It is also safeguarded by working relationships between the individual officer and prisoner, which are based upon trust rather than fear, cooperation as opposed to hostility, and upon communication as opposed to silence.

During the course of the field-work the uniformed staff revealed a considerable degree of discontent about what they considered to be the absence of an 'end product' to their work. Only one in ten of the officers thought that imprisonment acted to rehabilitate or deter offenders from re-offending. Instead the primary function of prison was seen to be that of containment, with the main role of the prison officer relegated to that of custodian. Thus, their sense of professionalism was bound up with the pride they could take in the smooth running of their own establishment. Goals associated with management and control, which assist the organizational efficiency of the institution, consequently became elevated to paramount importance at the expense of other types of organizational goals—such as the goal of racial equality.

It is not an unreasonable proposition that for governors, too, it is important to feel that as managers of the prison they are running a smooth ship. The primacy of this goal can be seen to have been reinforced by the distribution of a Circular Instruction in December 1984, which provided statements from the Prisons Board of both the tasks of the Prison Service and the functions of Prison Department establishments. What these statements are intended to provide is, 'the context within which individual establishments' tasks may be set, performance monitored and

[16] I. Dunbar (1985), *A Sense of Direction* (London: Home Office), 83.

account tendered'.[17] The tasks of the service were set out as follows:

The task of the Prison Service is to use with maximum efficiency the resources of staff, money, building and plant made available to it by Parliament in order to fulfil in accordance with the relevant provisions of the law, the following functions:

(*i*) to keep in custody untried or unsentenced prisoners, and to present them to court for trial or sentence;

(*ii*) to keep in custody, with such degree of security as is appropriate, having regard to the nature of the individual prisoner and his offence, sentenced prisoners for the duration of their sentence or for such shorter time as the Secretary of State may determine in cases where he has discretion;

(*iii*) to provide for prisoners as full a life as is consistent with the facts of custody, in particular making available the physical necessities of life; care for physical and mental health; advice and help with personal problems; work, education, training, physical exercise and recreation; and opportunity to practise their religion; and

(*iv*) to enable prisoners to retain links with the community and where possible assist them to prepare for their return to it.[18]

The functions of establishments are listed under six headings: custody of unsentenced prisoners; court commitment; custody of sentenced prisoners; security safety and control; services and facilities for prisoners; and community links and preparation for release. Functions which fall under the heading 'services and facilities for prisoners' constitute a fundamental statement of policy about the nature of regimes.[19] They spell out the requirement to supply basic amenities such as accommodation, meals, facilities for personal hygiene and sanitation, clothing, and opportunities for exercise. The provision of medical services for the diagnosis, treatment, and prevention of physical and mental disorders is also specified, as is help and advice to prisoners with any personal problems and the facilitation of their religious practices. Finally, establishments are expected to

---

[17] Home Office (1984), Prison Department Circular Instruction 55/1984, para. 4.

[18] Ibid., annex A.   [19] Ibid., para. 9 and annex B.

enable prisoners to spend the 'maximum possible time' out of their cells and to occupy prisoners as fully as possible in such activities as 'work, education, physical education, access to libraries and individual and collective leisure activities'.

Clearly in both of these statements from the Prisons Board the message being communicated about regimes is one which highlights the concrete and practical form which they should take. They make clear that whilst account will be taken of the availability of resources individual establishments will be assessed upon the provision and performance of these functions. What is not communicated is that there will be any review or evaluation of the purpose of the regime—in other words, the extent to which the functions are successful in serving a particular end.

The Circular does not deny this fact but unashamedly notes that the statements of tasks and functions are management tools and that they are practical rather than aspirational in nature. Aspirations, however, are not totally abandoned, 'The Prison Service must have a clear vision of the need to care for, to help and if possible to influence for the better the prisoners who are sent to it.[20] In his introduction to the 1984–5 on the Work of the Prison Department, the Director-General also notes:

The pursuit of greater efficiency and the improvement of management systems are not separate from the pursuit of humane and purposeful prison conditions, from the aim to improve the circumstances in which prisoners live, the care that can be given to them and the conditions in which our staff have to work: they are part of it.[21]

But what is the purpose of prison? What is meant by 'care for', 'help', 'if possible influence for the better'? Within a disciplined service it is perhaps understandable why prison staff focus upon the attainment of those goals which measurably demonstrate organizational efficiency. The two statements have clearly identified for them *what* is to be done. What they have not made clear is *why* they should be doing it.

[20] Ibid., para. 5.
[21] Home Office (1985), *Report on the Work of the Prison Department, 1984–5* (London: HMSO), para. 10.

5. THE WAY FORWARD

The problems which have been identified in implementing the department's race relations policy exemplify fundamental dilemmas within the Prison Service. Understatement of aspirational goals and the apparent continuance of what has been described as a 'moral vacuum' inevitably raise problems for the development and implementation of programmes, such as those concerned with race relations in prison, which have at their heart a concern with the quality of relationship between individual members of staff and prisoners. Essentially what is called for is a return to first principles: what are prisons for and how should they be run?

The primary decision to be made is whether prisons are to serve any purpose beyond that of containing prisoners in secure and physically decent conditions. Despite the diminution of faith in the rehabilitative ideal, concepts of treatment and training in custody are far from dead. Rule 1 of the Prison Rules remains:

The purpose of the training and treatment of convicted prisoners shall be to encourage and assist them to lead a good and useful life.[22]

Two problems which have dogged this approach, however, have been: first, the difficulties associated with translating abstract concepts into practice; and second, the complexity of defining adequate measures to assess achievement. One of the major reasons for disillusionment with the treatment model was that its success was measured solely in terms of reconviction rates.[23] As one author recently commented, 'In many ways such a measure was set up to fail the test.'[24] One way of interpreting Rule 1 would be to shift the emphasis from traditional notions of rehabilitation towards the concept of education in its broadest sense. In the same way that institutes of adult education are expected to provide students with exposure to a wide range of ideas, which they are then free to consider, prisons could provide prisoners with an opportunity to come into contact with

[22] Home Office (1983), *The Prison Rules 1964* (London (HMSO).

[23] R. Martinson (1974), 'What Works?—Questions and Answers about Prison Reform', *Public Interest*, Spring, 22–54.

[24] Dunbar, *A Sense of Direction*, p. 25.

alternative ways of looking at the world and at their own particular situation. Its measure of success would not hinge upon the reduction of criminal behaviour but would be gauged by the qualitative effects it had upon the regime and upon staff and prisoner morale. In many respects this approach has firm roots within the prison system. Many education departments already offer broad learning opportunities in such classes as social skills, and personal living patterns. Probation departments too have contributed by facilitating discussion forums and specialist groups to explore such problems as compulsive gambling, and drug and alcohol abuse. The difficulty is that many of these initiatives are uncoordinated and accorded a relatively low profile within individual establishments. They do not appear to represent a primary purpose which the organization is designed to serve.

If prisons are to serve such an educative function then the grey areas of the department's race relations policy become clarified in accordance with this. The primary aim of the policy would be to ensure not only the protection of basic human rights to decency, security, and equality of treatment, but also to foster racial tolerance and integration. If on the other hand, the only purpose which prisons are to serve is that of containing prisoners in tolerable physical conditions, then the goal of the race relations policy would be embodied in the protection of prisoners' rights and the avoidance of segregation.

Appendix

MEMBERS OF THE STEERING COMMITTEE

Ms PHILIPPA DREW Chairman until June 1985	P3 Division, Prison Department
Mr TONY BUTLER Chairman from June 1985	P3 Division, Prison Department
Mrs TRISH ATKINS	P3 Division, Prison Department
Mr LINCOLN CRAWFORD	Barrister-at-Law
Mr TREVOR HALL	Race Relations Consultant to the Home Office
Dr ROGER HOOD	Director, Centre for Criminological Research, University of Oxford; Fellow of All Souls College
Dr MANSUR LALLJEE	Staff Tutor in Psychology, Department of External Studies, University of Oxford
Professor JOHN REX	Director, Centre for Research in Ethnic Relations, University of Warwick
Miss ANGELA SMITH	P4 Division, Prison Department
Mr ROY WALMSLEY	Home Office Research and Planning Unit
Mr KEITH BANNISTER Secretary	P3 Division, Prison Department

Bibliography

Advisory Committee on Race Relations Research (1975), *Race Relations Research: A Report to the Home Secretary*, London: HMSO.

ALLEN, S. (1971), *New Minorities, Old Conflicts: Asian and West Indian Migrants in Britain*, London: Random House.

—— and SMITH, C. (1974), 'Race and Ethnicity in Class Formation: A Comparison of Asian and West Indian Workers', in F. Parkin (ed.), *The Social Analysis of Class Structure*, London: Tavistock.

—— BENTLEY, S., and BURNAT, J. (1977), *Work, Race and Immigration*, University of Bradford: School of Studies in Social Science.

AMOS, V., GILROY, P., and LAWRENCE, E. (1982), 'White Society, Black Struggle', in D. Robbins (ed.), *Rethinking Social Inequality*, Farnborough: Gower Press.

ANWAR, M. (1979), *The Myth of Return: Pakistanis in Britain*, London: Heinemann Educational Books.

—— (1986), *Race and Politics: Ethnic Minorities and the British Political System*, London: Tavistock.

BAGLEY, C., and VERMA, G. (1979), *Racial Prejudice, the Individual and Society*, Farnborough: Saxon House.

BAKER, J. R. (1974), *Race*, London: Oxford University Press.

BALLARD, C. (1979), 'Conflict, Continuity and Change', in V. S. Khan (ed.), *Minority Families in Britain*, London: Macmillan.

BANKS, J. A. (1981), *Multiethnic Education: Theory and Practice*, London: Allyn and Bacon.

BANTON, M. (1959), *White and Coloured: The Behaviour of British People Towards Coloured Immigrants*, London: Jonathan Cape.

—— (1967), *Race Relations*, London: Tavistock Publications Ltd.

—— (1972), *Racial Minorities*, London: Fontana.

—— (1977), *The Idea of Race*, London: Tavistock.

—— (1979), 'Analytical and Folk Concepts of Race and Ethnicity', *Ethnic and Racial Studies*, 2/2: 127–38.

—— (1983), *Racial and Ethnic Competition*, Cambridge: Cambridge University Press.

—— (1985), *Promoting Racial Harmony*, Cambridge: Cambridge University Press.

BARBER, A. (1985), 'Ethnic Origin and Economic Status', *Department of Employment Gazette*, 93: 467–77.

BARKER, M. (1981), *The New Racism*, London: Junction Books.

BARNES, H. E. and TEETERS, N. K. (1959), *New Horizons in Criminology*, Englewood Cliffs, NJ: Prentice Hall.

BARZUN, J. (1937), *Race: A Study in Superstition*, New York: Harcourt, Brace and Co.

BAXTER, P. and SANSOM, B. (eds.) (1972), *Race and Social Difference*, Harmondsworth: Penguin.

BECKER, H. (1958), 'Problems of Inference and Proof in Participant Observation', *American Sociological Review*, 23: 652–60.

BEN-TOVIM, G., and GABRIEL, J. (1979), 'The Politics of Race in Britain 1962–79', *Sage Race Relations Abstracts*, 4/4: 1–56.

—— GABRIEL, J., LAW, I., and STREDDER, K. (1986), *The Local Politics of Race*, London: Macmillian.

BENYON, J. (ed.) (1984), *Scarman and After: Essays Reflecting on Lord Scarman's Report, the Riots and their Aftermath*, Oxford: Pergamon.

BERK, B. (1966), 'Organisational Goals and Inmate Organisation', *American Journal of Sociology*, 71 (Mar.), 522–34.

BIDDISS, M. (ed.) (1979), *Images of Race*, Leicester: Leicester University Press.

BLALOCK, H. (1982), *Race and Ethnic Relations*, Englewood Cliffs, NJ: Prentice Hall.

BOWKER, G., and CARRIER, J. (eds.) (1976), *Race and Ethnic Relations*, London: Hutchinson.

BROWN, C. (1984), *Black and White Britain: The Third PSI Survey*, London: Heinemann.

BULLIVANT, B.(1981), *The Pluralist Dilemma in Education*, Sydney: Allen and Unwin.

BULMER, M. (1980), 'On the Feasibility of Identifying "Race" and "Ethnicity" in Censuses and Surveys', *New Community*, 8/1–2.

CALDWELL, W. (1968), 'A Survey of Attitudes toward Black Muslims in Prison', *Journal of Human Relations*, 16: 220–38.

CARROLL, L. (1974), *Hacks, Blacks and Cons*, Lexington, Mass.: Lexington Books, D. C. Heath and Co.

—— (1982), 'Race, Ethnicity, and the Social Order of the Prison', in R. Johnson and H. Toch (eds.), *The Pains of Imprisonment*, London: Sage.

CASHMORE, E. (1979), *Rastaman*, London: Allen and Unwin.

—— and TROYNA, B. (eds.) (1982), *Black Youth in Crisis*, London: Allen and Unwin.

—— —— (1983), *Introduction to Race Relations*, London: Routledge and Kegan Paul.

CLARKE, C., LEY, D., and PEACH, C. (eds.) (1984), *Geography and Ethnic Pluralism*, London: Allen and Unwin.

CLEMMER, D. (1940), *The Prison Community*, New York: Holt, Rinehart and Winston.

COLLINS, S. (1957), *Coloured Minorities in Britain: Studies in British Race Relations based on African, West Indian and Asiatic Immigrants*, London: Lutterworth Press.

Commission for Racial Equality (1986), *The Management of Race Relations Within Prison Establishments*, London: Commission for Racial Equality.

Committee of Inquiry into the Education of Children from Ethnic Minority Groups (1981), *West Indian Children in our Schools*, London: HMSO.

Committee on the Elimination of Racial Discrimination (1985), *Teaching, Education, Culture and Information as Means of Eliminating Racial Discrimi-*

nation: Implementation of the International Convention on the Elimination of all Forms of Racial Discrimination, Article 7, New York: United Nations.

Community Relations Commission (1977), *Urban Deprivation, Racial Inequality and Social Policy: A Report*, London: HMSO.

COWELL, D., JONES, T., and YOUNG, J. (eds.) (1982), *Policing the Riots*, London: Junction Books.

COX, O. C. (1948), *Caste, Class and Race: A Study of Social Dynamics*, New York: Doubleday.

—— (1976), *Race Relations: Elements and Dynamics*, Detroit, Ill.: Wayne State University Press.

CRESSEY, D. (1965), 'Prison Organisations', in J. G. March (ed.), *Handbook of Organisations*, Chicago: Rand McNally.

CROSS, M. (1982), 'Race and Social Policy: The Case of the CRE', in O. Stevenson and C. Jones (eds.), *Yearbook of Social Policy 1981*, London: Routledge and Kegan Paul.

CROW, I. (1987), 'Black People and Criminal Justice in the U.K.', *The Howard Journal of Criminal Justice*, 26/4 (Nov.), 303—14.

DAHYA, B. (1974), 'The Nature of Pakistani Ethnicity in Industrial Cities in Britain', in A. Cohen (ed.), *Urban Ethnicity (ASA Monograph 12)*, London: Tavistock, 77—117.

DANIEL, W. W. (1968), *Racial Discrimination in England*, Harmondsworth: Penguin.

DAVIDSON, T. (1974), *Chicano Prisoners: The Key to San Quentin*, New York: Holt, Rinehart and Winston.

DEAKIN, N. (1970), *Colour, Citizenship and British Society*, London: Panther Books.

—— and COHEN, B. G. (1970), 'Dispersal and Choice: Towards a Strategy for Ethnic Minorities in Britain', *Environment and Planning*, 2: 193–201.

Department of the Environment (1975), *Race Relations and Housing*, London: HMSO.

D'OREY, S. (1984), *Immigration Prisoners: A Forgotten Minority*, London: Runnymede Trust.

DUMMET, A., and DUMMET, M. (1969), 'The Role of Government in Britain's Racial Crisis', in L. Donnelly (ed.), *Justice First*, London: Sheed and Ward.

DUNBAR, I. (1985), *A Sense of Direction*, London: Home Office.

EDGAR, D. (1977), 'Racism, Fascism and the Politics of the National Front', *Race and Class*, 19/2: 111—31.

EDWARDS, J., and BATLEY, R. (1978), *The Politics of Positive Discrimination*, London: Tavistock.

Equal Opportunities Review (1987), Law Reports, 15 (Sept.—Oct.), 36—7.

EVANS, J. (1983), *Immigration Law*, London: Sweet and Maxwell.

FANON, F. (1967), *Black Skin, White Masks*, Harmondsworth: Penguin.

FARLEY, J. (1982), *Majority—Minority Relations*, Englewood Cliffs, NJ: Prentice Hall.

FIELD, S. (1984), *The Attitudes of Ethnic Minorities*, Home Office Research Study, No. 80, London: HMSO.

—— MAIR, G., REES, T., and STEVENS, P. (1981), *Ethnic Minorities in Britain: A Study of Trends in their Position since 1961*, Home Office Research Study, No. 68, London: HMSO.

FITZGERALD, M. (1977), *Prisoners in Revolt*, Harmondsworth: Pelican.

—— and SIM, J. (1979), *British Prisons*, Oxford: Basil Blackwell.

FLETT, H. (1982), 'Dimensions of Inequality: Birmingham Council Housing Allocations', *New Community*, 10/1 (summer).

FLUDGER, N. (1981), *Ethnic Minorities in Borstal*, London: Home Office, Prison Department, Directorate of Psychological Services.

FOOT, P. (1965), *Immigration and Race in British Politics*, Harmondsworth: Penguin.

—— (1969), *The Rise of Enoch Powell*, Harmondsworth: Penguin.

FOX, J. G. (1982), *Organizational and Racial Conflict in Maximum Security Prisons*, Lexington, Mass.: Lexington Books.

FOX, V. (1972), 'Racial Issues in Corrections', *American Journal of Corrections*, 34/6: 12—17.

FREEMAN, M. D., and SPENCER, S. (1979), 'The State, the Law and Race Relations in Britain Today', *Current Legal Problems*, 32: 117—42.

FRYER, P. (1984), *Staying Power: The History of Black People in Britain*, London: Pluto Press.

GARABEDIAN, P. (1963), 'Social Roles and Processes of Socialisation in the Prison Community', *Social Problems*, 11 (fall), 139—52.

GASKELL, G. (1986), 'Black Youth and the Police', *Policing.* 2/1: 26—34.

—— and SMITH, P. (1981), 'Are Young Blacks Really Alienated?', *New Society*, 14 May.

GESCHWENDER, J. A. (1977), *Class, Race and Worker Insurgency*, New York: Cambridge University Press.

GIALLOMBARDO, R. (1966), *Society of Women: A Study of Women's Prisons*, New York: John Wiley and Sons.

GILES, R. (1977), *The West Indian Experience in British Schools*, London: Heinemann.

GLASGOW, D. (1980), *The Black Underclass*, New York: Jossey Bass.

GLAZER, N., and MOYNIHAN, D. P. (1970), *Beyond the Melting Pot*, London: MIT Press.

—— (1975), *Affirmative Discrimination*, New York: Basic Books.

—— and MOYNIHAN, D. P. (eds.) (1975), *Ethnicity*, Cambridge, Mass.: Harvard University Press.

—— and YOUNG, K. (eds.) (1983), *Ethnic Pluralism and Public Policy*, London: Heinemann.

GOFFMAN, E. (1961), *Asylums*, Harmondsworth: Penguin.

GORDON, P. (1983), *White Law: Racism in the Police, Courts and Prisons*, London: Pluto Press.

—— (1984), *Deportations and Removal*, London: Runnymede Trust.

—— and KLUG, F. (1985), *British Immigration Control: A Brief Guide*, London: Runnymede Trust.

GOULBOURNE, S. (1985), *Minority Entry to the Legal Profession: A Discussion Paper* (Policy Papers in Ethnic Relations, 2), Coventry: Centre for Research in Ethnic Relations, University of Warwick.

GRANT, T., and MARTIN, I. (1982), *Immigration Law and Practice*, London: Cobden Trust.

GREGORY, J. (1987), *Sex, Race and the Law: Legislating for Equality*, London: Sage.

HALL, S., CRITCHER, C., JEFFERSON, T., CLARK, J., and ROBERTS, B. (1978), *Policing the Crisis: Mugging, the State and Law and Order*, London: Macmillan.

HIERNAUX, J. (1965), Introduction, 'The Moscow Expert Meeting', *International Social Science Journal*, 16/1, Paris: UNESCO

HIRO, D. (1973), *Black British, White British*, Harmondsworth: Penguin.

Home Affairs Committee (1980), *Racial Disadvantage 1980—1981*, London: HMSO.

—— (1981), *Commission for Racial Equality 1981—1982*, London: HMSO.

Home Office (1965), *Immigration from the Commonwealth*, London: HMSO.

—— (1977), *A Guide to the Race Relations Act 1976*, London: HMSO.

—— (1981*a*), Prison Department Circular Instruction, 28/1981.

—— (1981*b*), Prison Department Circular Instruction 28/1981, addendum 1.

—— (1981*c*), *Racial Attacks*, London: Home Office.

—— (1983*a*), Prison Department Circular Instruction 56/1983.

—— (1983*b*), *Report of Her Majesty's Chief Inspector of Prisons*, London: HMSO.

—— (1983*c*), *The Prison Rules 1964*, London: HMSO.

—— (1984), Prison Department Circular Instruction 55/1984.

—— (1985). *Report on the Work of the Prison Department, 1984—85*, London: HMSO.

—— (1986*a*), *The Ethnic Origin of Prisoners: The Prison Population on 30 June 1985 and Persons Received July 1984—March 1985*, Statistical Bulletin, 17/86.

—— (1986*b*), Prison Department Circular Instruction 32/1986.

—— (1987), *Prison Statistics, England and Wales 1986*, London: HMSO.

HOROWITZ, D. L. (1985), *Ethnic Groups in Conflict*, London: University of California Press.

HUSBAND, C. (ed.) (1982), *'Race' in Britain: Continuity and Change*, London: Hutchinson.

IANNI, F. (1974), *Black Mafia: Ethnic Succession in Organized Crime*, New York: Simon and Schuster.

IRWIN, J. (1970), *The Felon*, Englewood Cliffs, NJ: Prentice Hall.

—— (1977), 'The Changing Social Structure of the Man's Prison', in D. Greenberg (ed.), *Corrections and Punishment*, Beverley Hills, Calif.: Sage Publications.

—— and CRESSEY, D. R. (1982), 'Thieves, Convicts and the Inmate Culture', *Social Problems*, 10: 142—55.

JACKSON, P., and SMITH, S. (eds.) (1981), *Social Interaction and Ethnic Segregation*, London: Academic Press.

JACOBS, J. B. (1974), 'Street Gangs Behind Bars', *Social Problems*, 21/4 (winter).

—— (1975), 'Stratification and Conflict Among Prison Inmates', *Journal of Criminal Law and Criminology*, 66/4 (Dec.).

—— (1977), *Stateville: The Penitentiary in Mass Society*, Chicago: University of Chicago Press.

—— (1979), 'Race Relations and the Prisoner Sub-culture', in N. Norris and M. Tonry (eds.), *Crime and Justice: An Annual Review of Research*, Chicago: University of Chicago Press.

—— and KRAFT, L. (1978), 'Integrating the Keepers: A Comparison of Black and White Prison Guards in Illinois', *Social Problems*, 25: 304—18.

JOHNSON, R., and TOCH, H. (eds.) (1982), *The Pains of Imprisonment*, London: Sage.

JONES, C. (1977), *Immigration and Social Policy in Britain*, London: Tavistock.

JOSHUA, H., and WALLACE, T. (1983), *To Ride the Storm: The 1980 Bristol 'Riot' and the State*, London: Heinemann.

KANTROWITZ, N. (1969), 'The Vocabulary of Race Relations in a Prison', *Publication of the American Dialect Society*, 51: 23—34.

KARN, V. (1977/8), 'The Financing of Owneroccupation and its Impact on Ethnic Minorities', *New Community*, 6/1—2 (winter).

—— (1983), 'Race and Housing in Britain: The Role of the Major Institutions', in N. Glazer and K. Young (eds.), *Ethnic Pluralism and Public Policy*, London: Heinemann.

KERRIDGE, R. (1983), *Real Wicked Guy: A View of Black Britain*, Oxford: Basil Blackwell.

KETTLE, M. (1981), 'The Evolution of an Official Explanation', *New Society*, 3 Dec. 1981, 404—5.

KING, R. D., and ELLIOTT, K. W. (1977), *Albany: Birth of a Prison—End of an Era*, London: Routledge and Kegan Paul.

—— and MORGAN, R. (1976), *A Taste of Prison: Custodial Conditions for Trial and Remand Prisoners*, London: Routledge and Kegan Paul.

—— (1980), *The Future of the Prison System*, London: Gower.

KLUG, F., and GORDON, P. (1983), *Different Worlds: Racism and Discrimination in Britain*, London: Runnymede Trust.

LANDAU S. F. (1981), 'Juveniles and the Police', *British Journal of Criminology*, 21: 27—46.

—— and NATHAN, G. (1983), 'Selecting Delinquents for Cautioning in the London Metropolitan Area', *British Journal of Criminology*, 23: 28—49.

LAWRENCE, D. (1974), *Black Migrants, White Natives*, Cambridge: Cambridge University Press.

LAYTON-HENRY, Z. (1984), *The Politics of Race in Britain*, London: Allen and Unwin.

—— and RICH, P. B. (eds.) (1986), *Race, Government and Politics*, Basingstoke: Macmillan.

LIN, L. (1965), 'Verbal Attitudes and Overt Behaviour: A Study of Racial Discrimination', *Social Forces*, 43 (Mar.), 353—64.

LINCOLN, C. (1973), *The Black Muslims in America* (revised edn.), Boston: Beacon Press.

LITTLE, A. (1975), 'The Educational Achievement of Ethnic Minority Children in London Schools', in G. Verma and C. Bagley (eds.), *Race and Education Across Cultures*, London: Heinemann.

LITTLE, K. L. (1947), *Negroes in Britain: A Study of Racial Relations in English*

Society, London: Kegan Paul, Trench, Trubner and Co. Ltd.

LOFLAND, J. (1971), *Analysing Social Settings*, Belmont: Wadsworth.

LUSTGARTEN, L. (1980), *Legal Control of Racial Discrimination*, London: Macmillan.

MASON, D., and REX, J. (eds.) (1986), *Theories of Race and Ethnic Relations*, Cambridge: Cambridge University Press.

MCCONVILLE, S. (ed.), (1975), *The Use of Imprisonment: Essays in the Changing State of English Penal Policy*, London: Routledge and Kegan Paul.

MCCORKLE L., and KORN, R. (1954), 'Resocialisation Within the Walls', *Annals of the American Academy of Political and Social Science*, 293 (May), 88–98.

MCCREADY, W. C. (ed.) (1983), *Culture, Ethnicity and Identity: Current Issues in Research*, New York: Academic Press.

MCCRUDDEN, C. (1983), 'Anti-Discrimination Goals and the Legal Process', in N. Glazer and K. Young (eds.), *Ethnic Pluralism and Public Policy*, London: Heinemann.

MACDONALD, I. A. (1977), *Race Relations: The New Law*, London: Butterworths.

—— (1983), *Immigration Law and Practice*, London: Butterworths.

MCNEELY, R. L., and POPE, C. E. (eds.) (1981), *Race, Crime and Criminal Justice: Perspectives in Criminal Justice, ii*, Beverley Hills: Sage.

MARTINSON, R. (1974), 'What Works? Questions and Answers about Prison Reform', *Public Interest* (spring), 22–54.

MIAH, M. (1976), *Busing and the Black Struggle*, New York: Pathfinder Press.

MILES, R., and PHIZACKLEA, A. (1977), 'Class, Race, Ethnicity and Political Action', *Political Studies*, 15/4: 491–507.

—— —— (eds.) (1979), *Racism and Political Action in Britain*, London: Routledge and Kegan Paul.

MOONMAN, E. (1983), 'Race Relations: Understanding the Future', repr. from the *Journal of Royal Society of Arts* (Feb.).

MORRIS, M. D. (1975), *The Politics of Black America*, New York: Harper and Row.

MORRIS, T. P., MORRIS, P., and BARER, B. (1963), *Pentonville: A Sociological Study of an English Prison*, London: Routledge and Kegan Paul.

MORTIMORE, J., and BLACKSTONE, T. (1982), *Disadvantage and Education*, London: Heinemann Educational Books.

NACRO, Race Issues Advisory Committee (1986), *Black People and the Criminal Justice System*, London: NACRO.

—— (1988), *Some Facts and Findings about Black People in the Criminal Justice System*, NACRO briefing (June).

New Society (1982), *Race and Riots '81* (New Society Social Studies Reader), London: IPC.

New York State Special Commissions on Attica (1972), *Official Report*, New York: Bantam Books.

Office of Population Censuses and Surveys (1985), *Staff Attitudes in the Prison Service*, London: HMSO.

OWENS, C. E. (1980), *Mental Health and Black Offenders*, Gower, Mass.: Lexington Books.

172   *Race Relations in Prisons*

PATTERSON, S. (1965), *Dark Strangers*, Harmondsworth: Penguin.
PEACH, C. (1968), *West Indian Migration to Britain*, London: IRR/Oxford University Press.
—— (ed.) (1975), *Urban Social Segregation*, London: Longman.
—— ROBINSON, V., and SMITH, S. (eds.) (1981), *Ethnic Segregation in Cities*, London: Croom Helm.
PEARSON, D. G. (1981), *Race, Class and Political Activism*, Farnborough: Gower Press.
PHIZACKLEA, A., and MILES, R. (1980), *Labour and Racism*, London: Routledge and Kegan Paul.
PILKINGTON, A. (1984), *Race Relations in Britain*, Slough: University Tutorial Press.
PRYCE, K. (1979), *Endless Pressure*, Harmondsworth: Penguin.
RAINWATER, L. (1973), *Behind Ghetto Walls*, Harmondsworth: Penguin.
RATCLIFFE, P. (1981), *Racism and Reaction*, London: Routledge and Kegan Paul.
REEVES, F. (1983), *British Racial Discourse: A Study of British Political Discourse about Race and Race-Related Matters*, Cambridge: Cambridge University Press.
REX, J. (1970), 'The Concept of Race in Sociological Theory', in S. Zubaida (ed.), *Race and Racialism*, London: Tavistock.
—— (1973), *Race, Colonialism and the City*, London: Routledge & Kegan Paul.
—— (1981), *Social Conflict*, London: Longman.
—— (1983), *Race Relations in Sociological Theory* (2nd edn.), London: Routledge and Kegan Paul.
—— (1986), *Race and Ethnicity*, Milton Keynes: Open University Press.
—— and CROSS, M. (1982) *Unemployment and Racial Conflict in the Inner City*, Birmingham: Research Unit on Ethnic Relations.
—— and MOORE, R. (1967), *Race, Community and Conflict: A Study of Sparkbrook*, London: Oxford University Press.
—— and TOMLINSON, S. (1979), *Colonial Immigrants in a British City*, London: Routledge and Kegan Paul.
RICHMOND, A. H. (1988), *Immigration and Ethnic Conflict*, London: Macmillan.
ROBINSON, V. (1986), *Transients, Settlers and Refugees: Asians in Britain*, Oxford: Clarendon Press.
ROSE, E. J. B., et al. (1969), *Colour and Citizenship*, London: Institute of Race Relations/Oxford University Press.
ROTHMAN, D. (1971), *The Discovery of the Asylum: Social Order and Disorder in the Republic*, Boston: Little Brown.
Runnymede Trust and Radical Race Statistics Group (1980), *Britain's Black Population*, London: Heinemann Educational Books.
RUSCHE, G., and KIRCHHEIMER, O. (1939), *Punishment and Social Structure*, New York: Columbia University Press.
SCARMAN, the Rt. Hon. Lord, OBE (1981), *The Scarman Report: The Brixton Disorders 10–12 April 1981*, London: Penguin.
SHAW, J. (1985), 'Race Relations Training Seminars', *Prison Service Journal*, 8–11 July.
SIVANANDAN, A. (1981–2), 'From Resistance to Rebellion: Asian and Afro

Caribbean Struggles in Britain', *Race and Class*, 23/2—3: 111—52.

—— (1982), *A Different Hunger: Writings on Black Resistance*, London: Pluto Press.

SMITH, D. J. (1977), *Racial Disadvantage in Britain* (the PEP Report), Harmondsworth: Penguin.

—— and GRAY, J. (1983), *Police and People in London: The Police in Action*, iv, London: Policy Studies Institute.

SMITH, T. E. (1981), *Commonwealth Migration: Flows and Policies*, London: Macmillan.

STERN, V. (1987), *Bricks of Shame*, Harmondsworth: Penguin.

STEVENS, P., and WILLIS, C. F. (1979), *Race, Crime and Arrests* (Home Office Research Study No. 58), London: HMSO.

STONE, J. (1985), *Racial Conflict in Contemporary Society*, London: Fontana.

SYKES, G. M. (1958), *Society of Captives: A Study of a Maximum Security Prison*, Princeton, NJ: Princeton University Press.

—— and MESSINGER, S. M. (1960), 'The Inmate Social System', *Theoretical Studies in Social Organisation of the Prison* (Pamphlet No. 15), New York: Social Science Research Council, 13—19.

THOMAS, C. W., and FOSTER, S. C. (1973), 'The Importation Model of Inmate Social Roles: An Empirical Test', *The Sociological Quarterly*, 14 (spring), 226—34.

TIERNEY, J. (ed.) (1982), *Race, Migration and Schooling*, London: Holt, Rinehart and Winston.

TOMLINSON, S. (1980), 'The Educational Performance of Ethnic Minority Children', *New Community*, 8/3: 213—43.

TROYNA, B. (1983), ' "A Question of Numbers": Race Relations, Social Policy and the Media', in P. Golding (ed.), *Mass Media and Social Policy*, Oxford: Martin Robertson.

TUCK, M., and SOUTHGATE, P. (1981), *Ethnic Minorities, Crime and Policing: A Survey of the Experiences of West Indians and Whites* (Home Office Research Study No. 70), London: HMSO.

UNESCO (1983), *'Racism', Science and Pseudo-Science: Proceedings of the Symposium to Examine Pseudo-Scientific Theories Invoked to Justify Racism and Racial Discrimination', Athens 1981*, Paris: Unesco.

United Nations, Committee on the Elimination of Racial Discrimination (1986), 'Positive Measures Designed to Eradicate all Incitement to, or Acts of, Racial Discrimination: Implementation of the International Convention on the Elimination of All Forms of Racial Discrimination', Article 4, New York: United Nations.

VAN DEN BERGH, P. (1978), *Race and Racism*, New York: John Wiley.

VESSUP, A. (1983), *Symbolic Communication: Understanding Racial Stereotypes that Persist*, Elgin, Ill.: Elgin Community College.

WARD, D., and KASSEBAUM, G. (1965), *Women's Prison: Sex and Social Structure*, Chicago: Aldine.

WATSON, J. L. (ed.) (1977), *Between Two Cultures: Migrants and Minorities in Britain*, Oxford: Basil Blackwell.

WELLMAN, D. T. (1977), *Portraits of White Racism*, London: Cambridge University Press.

WILLIS, C. (1983), *The Use, Effectiveness and Impact of Police Stop and Search Powers* (Home Office Research and Planning Unit Paper No. 15), London: HMSO.

WILSON, W. J. (1976), *Power, Racism and Privilege*, New York: Free Press.

World Conference to Combat Racism and Racial Discrimination (1983), *Report of the Second World Conference to Combat Racism and Racial Discrimination*, New York: United Nations.

Glossary

Baron   Prison argot for one who achieves power within the inmate hierarchy by means of exploitative activities within the illicit economy. Specifically involving the lending of money or the lending or selling of tobacco or drugs.

Board of Visitors   Appointed by the Home Secretary to oversee the administration of the establishment and the treatment of the inmates; and to conduct adjudications on the more serious breaches of prison discipline. They are not part of the management structure of the Prison Service but act as an independent watchdog.

Dispersal Prisons   Maximum security training establishments for long-term prisoners which are designed to hold amongst their populations men who are deemed to be of the highest security risk.

Doing Bird   Prison argot for serving a sentence.

F1150 File   The main record kept on each prisoner which serves as the primary source of documentary information on a prisoner's social, criminal and prison background.

Hooch   An alcoholic beverage illicitly brewed by prisoners.

Local Prisons   Responsible for the initial assessment and classification and allocation of convicted prisoners, obtaining information about their backgrounds and identifying their particular needs.

Local Review Committee   Appointed by the Home Secretary to review and report to him on the suitability for early release on parole licence of every eligible prisoner. Every Prison Department establishment holding or likely to hold parole-eligible prisoners has a Local Review Committee.

Orderly Jobs   Positions of limited or qualified trust which often involve prisoners working closely with prison staff in specific areas of the prison such as the reception unit, the administrative block or the gymnasium.

Peter   Prison argot for cell.

Prison Inspectorate   Statutory body, independent of the Prison Department, headed by Her Majesty's Chief Inspector of Prisons. The appointment of Chief Inspector is made by the Crown on the advice of the Home Secretary. His duty is to inspect and report on prison conditions and the treatment of prisoners in individual establishments and where necessary undertake thematic reviews.

Prisons Board The board of directors of the Prison Department.

Rule 43 Permits the segregation of prisoners for their own protection or because they are deemed to represent a threat to good order and discipline (Rule 46 in young offender establishments).

Screw Prisoner terminology for a prison officer.

Taxing Prison argot referring to the extraction of interest on the sale of goods and the provision of loans and services.

Youth Custody Centres Accommodate convicted young offenders between the ages of 15 and 21, who have been sentenced to a normal minimum term of more than 4 months.

Index

GLASGOW UNIVERSITY
LAW LIBRARY